Anger: Surviving Toxic Relationships

Anger: Surviving Toxic Relationships

TWENTY-SEVEN ANGRY COUNSELING CASES RESOLVED

Carol L. Rhodes PhD

ISBN-13: 9781547248988
ISBN-10: 154724898X
Library of Congress Control Number: 2017909214
CreateSpace Independent Publishing Platform
North Charleston, South Carolina

Also by Carol L. Rhodes, PhD:
    Why Women and Men Don't Get Along (with Norman S. Goldner)
    Affairs: Emergency Tactics
    I'm Just Not Happy

Thank you to the Morningside Writing Group in Port St. Lucie, Florida. Your editing and encouragement have been invaluable.

Contents

Introduction

The first, second, third, and fourth parts of this book describe several couples' counseling cases in which anger was acted out verbally, physically, and even silently. The history of family dynamics that set up angry personalities and solutions for each case are detailed, as well as the therapy outcomes. Part 5 provides a personal seven-day action plan, which individuals can use to take charge of themselves inside or outside of their angry relationships.

Part 1 demonstrates marriage-counseling cases in which people express anger in a variety of negative ways, and it details the effects that behavior has on intimate relationships. These angry individuals are wedded to their anger; moreover, they enjoy expressing anger and use any opportunity to verbalize their hateful, pent-up feelings.

Part 1 also includes solutions for angry people who have grown tired of feeling and acting out of control. Though dealing with anger through emotional outbursts may temporarily relieve inner agitation and tension, angry individuals, once they mature, will realize that their angry tirades are not in their best interest.

Part 2 illuminates the confusion, frustration, and anger created when people live with either a passive, passive/aggressive, impulsive, silent, or narcissistic personality. These individuals are unable to express anger in a healthy way and, in many cases, do not realize they are angry. Consequently, anger is acted out in a mixture of indirect and hostile behaviors—these people may respond slowly or not at all, may act sullen, may repeatedly fail to accomplish promised tasks, and may act out impulsively. What these people say and what they do are two different things—they cannot share their true feelings.

Part 3 portrays angry, destructive ways of communicating in relationships: sarcasm, contempt, criticism, and silence. The section on how to successfully resolve relationships describes how to handle verbal assaults, emotional turmoil, and the effects of demeaning interactions.

Part 4 briefly presents therapy examples of individuals whose habitual communication consists of distortion, dissociation, personalization, and narcissism. These individuals' partners are often baffled and angered by the unrealistic, off-the-mark, and surreal communication. This type of communication often dissolves the relationships' connections. Sorting out the emotional gibberish is difficult but can be done, and satisfaction in life depends on clarification.

Part 5 details the seven-step plan to gaining satisfaction and happiness in relationships.

PART ONE

Acted-Out Anger

CHAPTER 1

Understanding and Managing Anger

Rachel, a thirty-four-year-old architect, began her third marriage-counseling session without her husband, Matt, who said the following when we ended the second session: "I don't have issues with anger, and I don't need counseling—Rachel does."

Rachel

Leaning forward on the couch in my office, squeezing her hands together, Rachel described her husband's latest angry explosion.

"Bang! I was standing in the kitchen, and my heart started to pound. My stomach felt queasy, and I couldn't breathe. My husband walked in, slammed the door, and glared at me. He was practically growling. With a loud, accusatory voice, he said, 'Do you realize you parked your car two inches from the garbage cans? Are you crazy?'

"An hour of yelling began. He repeatedly put me down and banged on the table and then…silence for the rest of the evening. If I had said one word, he would have picked up where he had left off. His hateful behavior disappeared into thin air, as though it had never happened."

Fumbling in her purse for a tissue, she said, "I can't stand it, but I can't stop him!"

Rachel's experience with her angry husband was not unusual in its content or in the silence that followed.

Anger

Anger demands attention right now. When you live with an angry person, you know that everything may come to a stop, and you can only cringe, watch your partner's sneering, and listen to his or her screaming, shouting, or loud disciplinary talk—which you've heard before. Or the punishment may be silence acted out for hours, days, or weeks. When it is over, you are the one who is to blame, who failed in some way. Your partner is never wrong, but if a "sorry" pops up, it means nothing because the agitation is already building for the next bout of anger.

Your partner's anger permeates your life; it is no longer a simple spike into consciousness or a one-time event. Whenever your partner walks into the house, you become alert, just like Rachel. You check his or her face for a particular look, a disagreeable pursing of the lips, or an agitated tone. Anger dominates the relationship, you constantly fear eruptions. You learn to fearfully step back and act cautious; you do not bother to intellectually clarify and handle the emotional flood that overtakes your system.

There are times when anger is a natural reaction that stems from the brain's amygdala, an emotional subsection of the brain. For instance, an individual is expected to act angry when faced with a person who goads, attacks his or her character, or persists in obnoxious actions. In relationships, people use anger when they take opportunities through words or deeds to chastise, humiliate, and attack their partner. Their doing so discourages intimacy and a peaceful coexistence.

Freedom to be open and honest, to be yourself, disappears. To the world you present yourself and your relationship as stable and positive; your troubled real life is kept a troubled secret. Eager to appear normal and happy, you are ashamed to reveal your angst to others. You are disgusted, confused, and often fearful of your partner's unconscionable behavior.

Loving children, loyal friends, and successful careers cannot make up for the chaos, loneliness, and pain suffered when you are caught in the emotional web of your partner's anger.

Part 1 will help you to achieve two goals: first, you will understand why you chose an angry person and remain anger's victim; second, you will learn to take charge and to change your inner and outer reactions to both subtle and overt anger attacks.

Altering your experience requires courage since even thinking about change can be frightening. It is easier to put up with the known (such as painful relationships) rather than delve into the murky waters of the unknown self or summon the courage to confront your angry partner. Knowledge will set you free. Knowledge will clarify why you are participating in an abusive relationship when you feel trapped and disturbed. Knowledge will help you make an informed decision and take effective action.

The Angry Partner

Anger intended to control you and your actions is insidious, a low-level form of interacting that can slyly infiltrate your relationship. While anger slips and slides into your life, you try to adapt to your partner's unacceptable behavior and ugly words by making excuses. You may say things like "his boss is impossible" or "she's on edge because she works too many hours" or "it's my fault—I should have been more understanding." Or you may try to solve the problem by saying things like "he's right—I seldom cook what he wants, and that has to change" or "next time, I'll let her know my mother will be stopping by so that she can prepare" or "I guess I'm too demanding sexually."

Despite your efforts, the unexpected and unnecessary anger continues.

Anger Patterns

In the presence of a partner who displays either overt or covert anger, emotions are difficult to manage and any response becomes fodder for anger. In general, displays of overt anger are expressed with unacceptable, in-your-face behaviors that are physical or verbal or both. Covert anger flies under the radar and is difficult to tease out of an interaction.

Understanding your partner's anger patterns will shed light on specific forms of angry behavior and will shift emotional reactions of fear and confusion to the calm of the intellect. For example, if you had an autistic child, it would be in your best interest to learn how to understand and help that child, not to continuously struggle and expect the child to be different. In a similar manner, it is in your best interest to recognize anger patterns. Your doing so will provide the emotional and intellectual tools needed to calmly combat your partner's anger.

The following are the most-common anger patterns:

- Out-of-the-blue anger erupts when you least expect it. There is no rational explanation.
- Threatening anger is expressed in a variety of ways. Your partner may wag his or her finger, glare at you, roll his or her fists, invade your personal space, threaten to push you, make nasty personal comments, or speak with a commanding or scathing voice. This behavior is meant to frighten and tear your self-esteem to bits.

- When tit-for-tat anger is expressed, you and your partner must play the game together, and a general theme is followed: my anger is worse than your anger.
- Specific repetitive anger is expressed when one issue cannot be resolved, causing the relationship to unravel.
- Intense repetitive anger is meant to punish, educate, and control a partner's behavior.
- When anger is turned against the self, the recipient of the anger takes the blame for his or her partner's anger.
- Manipulative anger occurs when particular issues ignite an explosion related to money, sex, family, politics, religion, or any sensitive arena.
- Anger solves problems. A relationship issue needs airing but the angry partner always has the right solution to every problem; he or she stops any mutual discussions. You are wrong; he or she is right.
- Retrospective anger begins with a notable silence. After thinking over a verbal exchange or situation, these partners distort what has been said and become offended and angry.
- Anger is used as a communication style. Any discussion attempt is met with bubbling or explosive anger that has been lurking beneath a thin-skinned angry surface.
- Walking-in-the-door anger is anger that has been brewing during the day and particularly on the commute home. Drive time revives historical, weekend or imaginary grievances.
- Trigger anger is anger that flares up in a second for no reason.

People who use anger to control and demean others justify their behavior. For example, angry attackers may claim that outbursts are not under their control; therefore, they are not to blame. This type of refusal to accept responsibility is similar to a plea of temporary insanity in a courtroom.

If you don't get over the disturbance caused by their outburst, you may hear something like this: "There you go again—you don't understand. You make matters worse because you twist everything around." In other words, the victims are always at fault and are responsible for the verbal assaults. If the victims of this anger attempt to disengage, their partners will follow them out of the room. Their anger will intensify if the victims try to explain their intellectual or emotional responses, and the angry partners will certainly discuss who is responsible—the victims.

These patterns of anger and rage are akin to the buildup of static electricity, which usually is discharged at the nearest target. Your words, behavior, and character actually have little to do with these attacks, just as the tree struck by lightning did nothing to attract the electrical charge.

Fear of your partner's flare-ups, nasty words, criticism, sarcasm, unacceptable behavior, and periods of silence becomes the status quo. You may realize that you are in an undeclared war of anger and that you are living with the enemy!

To wage war against anger requires not only mental and physical training but also a plan. You need strategies.

Solutions

Do not permit anger to wear you down and batter your self-esteem. Any conversation with an angry person can be turned into an attack or a negative question and answer session. When your free time is spent trying to understand what has been said or implied about your stupidity, your lack of skills, or the fact that you never do anything right, you are in an anger-based relationship. Bruised and battered, you repeatedly try to gather your emotional forces but are attacked again and again and prevented from fully recovering.

Stop. Step back. You are being beaten down and controlled; you have been pulled into an orbit where you are reacting exactly as your partner desires. His or her anger is governing you because you are letting it do so.

You are just as powerful as your partner and just as strong willed; moreover, you can be just as persistent in the face of irrational anger as your abusive partner is in bullying you. Expecting you to fold, your partner allows the angry, powerful presentation to roll on, gains strength and becomes seemingly invincible. So what? You will become strong and invincible the minute you quit giving in and giving up.

Instead of trying to manage anger as the trapped reactor, you become the powerful handler of anger because you know what you are dealing with and what to expect when anger strikes. This may sound impossible, but it is doable.

You learn to problem solve, to seriously contemplate past incidents of anger, to analyze the relevant patterns, and to plan and practice your responses. When you see and hear the angry rumbles begin, you will be able to let your intellect take over instead of fear because you have prepared yourself. Once equipped with knowledge and resolve, you decide how the bouts of anger proceed.

You learn to step into the fray calmly; you do not have to step fearfully away whenever your angered partner wants or expects you to. Instead of experiencing the emotional contagion of angry words, distorted facial expressions, or threatening body language—all of which may cause your heart to accelerate and your blood pressure to go up—you learn how to handle the situation. You must mentally practice how to handle your partner's anger, and you must learn to view such behavior as absurd, ridiculous, and infantile.

Here is another option: deliberately, calmly, and purposefully step out of the room and thus out of reach. If you are forcefully restrained, call for help. Do not allow physical interference. It is critical—even though you may fear retaliation—that you show backbone.

Keep this codicil in mind: if you cannot step out of a room without incident, you are living with physical abuse. Physical abuse is an entirely different situation; anger often foreshadows assault. When physical abuse occurs, you should seek immediate help. Let your family, church officials, police, or family services know. Do not allow even a hint of anger-based physical activity to begin. Tell the world, and do not be embarrassed.

You may find yourself in shock and unsure of what to make of physical abuse, or when physical abuse first occurs, you may think it to be a one-time indiscretion, such as a slap, a push, or a poke that results in bruising. The beginning of physical abuse requires *touch*, so do not touch your partner or allow him or her to touch you under any anger-related circumstances!

Action

Although you may recognize a particular anger style, the lines often blur. For example, a word may spark out-of-the-blue anger that morphs into a habitual form of rage because a sensitive subject, such as money, gets brought up.

You may feel that putting up with out-of-control behavior is demeaning because you know you should somehow take charge. Perhaps you have tried repeatedly and in a variety of ways to alter these episodes, only to find that nothing seems to work, that things are getting worse, not better. If that is your situation, your choices are the following:

- Continue to think the same thoughts that leave the problems unsolved
- Learn to endure, give up your dreams, and live an angst-filled relationship (perhaps for the sake of your children)
- Leave the relationship

Or you can refine your understanding of yourself, your partner, and your situation; once you understand everything, you learn to utilize new methods for reaching your goals. I recommend that path. By studying the action-oriented methods revealed in the following chapters, you will learn to take charge of the disrespect and anger directed toward you. If you practice the provided techniques and learn to apply them, your relationship will either improve or be exposed for what it truly is—irremediable.

The following chapters reveal the art of disengaging and altering the status quo.

CHAPTER 2
Out-of-The-Blue Anger

Anger can reverberate from one generation to another like a family tradition, shaping conflicts into an emotional disease. Fathers or mothers whose angry explosions manage their households and create fear teach their children how feelings are handled, either as an angry reaction to actual situations or angry reactions to thoughts that come to mind.

If you were brought up in an angry family, real feelings and issues were not discussed. You learned to be vigilant, and that means you had to walk on eggshells, fearing that if you talked about true thoughts and feelings, the anger bombs would burst.

The Angry Wife

Disagreements with an angry partner are multiplied when partners, rather than face the issues at hand, retreat to their arsenal of dysfunctional reactions: criticism, sarcasm, and threats. Either these angry flare-ups include the children, or there is no attempt to keep them out of hearing range.

Family relationship-management techniques become etched into children's minds and are automatically repeated when they grow up and find partner-victims or people who beat them up psychologically.

In the following story, Pat never viewed her anger as a problem; she simply "got things off her chest." She had learned in her family that the person who throws the first punch survives. Consequently, when her husband told her that he refused to listen to another angry outburst and wanted a divorce, she thought he must be having a nervous breakdown or an affair. His decision, she thought, certainly was not because she preferred to air her feelings in an honest manner.

Pat

In my office for her first counseling session, Pat squirmed, crossing and recrossing her legs, but eventually settled down. She stared at me as she said, "My husband says he is done with our marriage. 'It's over. *Fini!*' He can no longer handle my behavior toward him."

As she spoke about the end of her marriage, I did not detect distress. Instead, it was as if she were talking about a fictional character.

With eyes still glued on me, speaking in a whispery, confidential voice, Pat shifted from her marriage and began to ask me questions about my life, questions I assumed were a way to allay her anxiety. I changed the focus by asking her to tell me about herself.

"I always view the glass as half-full rather than half-empty; in fact, I hope someday to be a motivational speaker."

That was the yin, and the yang came next. Pat came to therapy because though she saw herself as a positive person, she tore her husband down at every opportunity. "I don't know why I do it. I loathe him one minute and love him the next.

"My husband says he wants a divorce because *I* am out of control. That is absolutely untrue! I need an expert to help him understand that anger is natural. I occasionally get angry but do so with good reason. Doesn't every marriage have its arguments?"

Instead of acknowledging her husband's disturbed reaction to her anger, Pat was dismissing his feelings with the implication that he could not handle the anger, in the sense that he was overly sensitive and did not understand the nature of relationships.

As Pat's thoughts raced into consciousness, her mind was like a leaf caught in the wind: she expressed angry, scrambled thoughts about her husband without thoughtful consideration. Her conscious mind told her that she loved her husband, Jim, and wanted the marriage, but it seemed that a mysterious force took her over when she declared she could not help her negative thoughts and angry outbursts.

The Angry Family

Pat's marriage began peacefully when the new couple moved to the West Coast, away from her contentious, mean-spirited family. They had an opportunity to establish a relationship focused on each other, and Pat reported that those early days "were the happiest times of my life."

They had lived in California for seven years when Jim was transferred back to Michigan. After they moved back to Michigan, their interactions with Pat's original family triggered the slippery slide into marital misery.

Pat's History

Pat told me her parents had been separated, not divorced, for fifteen years because of vicious, nasty arguments. Her five siblings were pessimistic and moody, and they put each other down at every opportunity, though in a jolly fashion. (Can people put each other down in a jolly fashion? I don't think so.) Pat saw her family's style of interacting. She said she knew better than to repeat it. She knew Jim was not a horrible person who deserved to be attacked. She knew her behavior was not justified, but she could not help herself.

In essence, Pat had transferred her childhood fears onto her husband, fears with octopus-like arms. As her parents tore themselves to bits emotionally and physically, no one had her back when she was young. She recalled the passion of her parents' anger, describing it as horrific. She said that they threatened each other with divorce, physical harm, and financial ruin. They slashed at each other's core personality. Those authoritative parents eventually directed their anger and sarcasm to their kids, generating experiences and memories that left open wounds in the psyches of Pat and her siblings.

When Pat's husband talked to her in an authoritative style, she became the fearful child again. Each time she lashed out to silence Jim, her experience of "power over" was reinforced. *Power-over* is when people believe they have the ability to make others do what they want, and that belief makes them feel in command. Pat felt satisfaction with power-over and often had thoughts similar to the following: "I was right. I have to let him know how I feel. He can't get away with talking to me like that!" However, Pat's indulging in such comforting messages was what kept her impaled on her own anger.

Transference

A retreat to childhood experiences is something psychologists call transference. Whenever Pat treated her husband as the enemy, she was transferring feelings she had toward others in the past to her husband. She identified with the aggressors, her parents, by becoming critical and sarcastic. Instead of feeling emotionally vulnerable as she did when a child, Pat often turned her fear into rage and used it to terrorize her husband.

Out-of-control anger is a habit. Because Pat had been on autopilot and had stopped paying attention to what she was doing or how Jim was responding, she failed to notice the ultimate bad results and, in fact, justified them.

Is Change Possible?

When a particular behavior is reinforced, it persists. When it is not reinforced, it eventually ceases to exist. In Pat's case, she reinforced her pattern of out-of-the-blue anger with her internal dialogue. "I have to tell him how I feel!" she would think. Then she would feel satisfied when her husband appeared powerless in the face of her rage.

Pat indicated that she wanted to stay married and wanted to change, but I wonder if she was capable of self-reflection. Could she stand back and look at her thoughts, words, and behavior *and* control her angry attitude?

Progress in therapy was dependent upon Pat's ability grasp the significance of the following issues:

1. Can Pat acknowledge that her emotional hurricanes are a result of childhood defenses meant to ward off feelings of being afraid, defenseless, criticized, and ignored.
2. Could she understand that she was reacting to her own dramatic internal dialogue?
3. Was she motivated to change, or was she in therapy simply to indicate to her husband that she will be different?

Pat's personality style was intense and passionate. Her self-dialogue was inflammatory. Some of the least noxious words she would say to herself resembled the following comment: "I cannot stand Jim when he looks at me like that. Why would he say that? How stupid! He's deliberately goading me."

Pat said that whenever she was angry and expressed her feelings, she felt good—great, in fact. Her rage always felt justified. She was exhilarated by her negative passion, her rightness reinforced. Pat's primitive, emotional self needed to release her self-righteous anger.

Help was on the way as Pat watched her two sons' angry behavior. Pat indicated to me that everything was love-love when she was parenting her sons, but her two sons naturally mimicked Pat's anger when they were upset. Large teenage boys expressing rage can be scary.

I suggested that instead of reacting to her sons' anger with more of the same behavior and irate indignation, she should view her sons' anger as a reflection of her own out-of-control emotions. Pat was able to step back objectively and look at herself through her sons' eyes. She saw her ugly behavior, and her doing so seemed to help shift her angry thought patterns.

I also suggested that whenever Pat felt a surge of anger use the one-minute rule to immediately control herself and to alter her thoughts and feelings. I told her that her doing so would be difficult but doable.

One-Minute Rule

The one-minute rule is a powerful technique of thought rerouting you can use to get yourself under control. Stop whatever you are thinking for one minute (check your watch or do something similar), take three deep breaths, and say, "I feel calm." After a few calming words, you will notice your mind wanting to dart away into old thoughts. That is not a problem; just toss out the diversionary thought and immediately repeat, "I am calm." You will feel the calming effect after one minute. Be patient because filling up a minute takes about forty repetitions. (To ease into the one-minute rule, you may need to apply a thirty-second rule as a first step.)

Anger does not have to be vented. I suggested to Pat that whenever she was flooded with anger, use the one-minute rule and then muffle herself for ten minutes. The main goal was to stop, think about her thoughts, and take control of whatever was going on in her mind.

Feelings originate from a trigger, but what is a trigger? Is it real or is it a flash from the past? Has your husband just done something that is offensive? If so, spitting out hateful words does not solve the problem. He simply feels and hears the poison.

Take charge of yourself! Settle down, calm your mind, and talk in a normal tone. To help bring calming ideas to your mind, memorize the following concepts:

- Angry thoughts are driven by habit. Do they mean anything? Stop and decide whether you want to entertain them. If not, redirect your thoughts. Set a timer for one minute. In that time, continuously repeat something similar to "I love Jim" or "Jim is my friend," and completely focus on the words.
- You are not the victim of your mind. If a thought or feeling comes to mind, so what? You have sixty thousand thoughts a day, but are they all meaningful?
- Change your physiology for ten minutes or longer: immediately take physical action. Take a deep breath, cut the grass, walk outside, run around the block, do floor exercises, do jumping jacks, or jump rope. Physical activity calms the system and elevates the mind.
- Another option is to write "I feel calm; I am calm" ten times. Later, if your anger continues to rumble, speak to your husband in a modulated voice about your feelings—if they make sense. Remember that you *do not* have to verbalize every thought and feeling.

Anger is an infection, poisonous to you and to the family system. You will enter a process of healing by therapeutically investigating your inner conflict and by eliminating the repetition of the transference. Regurgitating every thought is ridiculous. As a motivational speaker, you would not become irate at an audience member's comment. In social situations, you do not say everything that comes to mind. Use the same control with your partner. Feeling angry is a green light. You may feel that you have the right to say anything to your partner because you are angry and he or she made you angry. You feel powerful when you spew anger. You demolish your partner. Your ego goes up; your partner's goes down.

Ask yourself this crucial question: do you get what you want when you are nasty? Perhaps you feel that you get wanted distance from your partner when you express your anger. Perhaps you feel that you do not need to interact with your partner and that you get rid of the tension when you succumb to your anger. Perhaps acting nasty makes you feel powerful. In any of those cases, take yourself seriously and quit acting as if your thoughts meant anything about your partner or another person. Those feelings are all about you.

Pat's children were not immune to her fits of anger and rage. Her children undoubtedly experienced fear when she expressed rage toward their father, and they learned to manage themselves with anger. Since we are learning machines at every age, Pat can now help her sons learn new behavior by altering her actions toward her husband.

Jim

Jim, Pat's husband, came to a session several months into Pat's therapy and said the person he had married eighteen years ago was back. He also said, "I'm happy and the household is peaceful," but he did not trust that Pat's positive behavior would continue.

Jim and I had some work to do. When Pat eliminated her angry style, Jim was naturally afraid that she would do a 180-degree turn if he accepted her proclamation that she had changed. I felt his fears were natural; however, such unnecessary trepidation might contaminate the positive strides in their relationship.

Dealing with an Angry Person

Jim had used a variety of techniques to handle Pat's anger. None solved the problem. The following list comprises different types of comments he would make while trying to act out certain roles.

- The authority: "You are a frustrated housewife. You could not survive without me."
- The psychologist: "Do you understand the psychological damage you cause your sons when you scream?"
- The boss: "You are not to say or do that again."
- The victim: "There you go again."
- Feeding the past: "Well, you are acting just like your father."

The point of Jim's therapy was to alert him to habitual thoughts that produced words and behavior antithetical to his desire to reestablish a good relationship. Being vigilant to his thoughts was necessary to prevent old ideas from naturally falling into place and contaminating goals.

For a person to consciously live in the moment, he or she must grab old thoughts and toss them. Old thoughts are like chewing on gristle. Just chew, chew, chew as though you like gristle and it was nutritional. Stuffing your mouth full of gristle would be painful, and chewing on old habitual thoughts is no different.

Six months after their therapy ended, Pat and Jim reported a huge improvement in their life together, but since the pull from the past is profoundly addictive, we continually schedule follow-up sessions, in which they remind themselves to stay on a positive track and examine any new issues that arise.

CHAPTER 3
Threatening Anger

T hreatening anger includes wagging fingers, glaring, contorting faces in hateful ways, speaking with a commanding or scathing voice, and invading personal space—all of which is meant to frighten. Whether this abuse occurs once a day or once a month, it should not be tolerated.

An Abusive Marriage
Peace at any cost was Emily's motto. In order to keep peace, Emily learned in her first year of marriage to avoid reacting not only to the nasty words of her husband, Jerry, but also to his threatening behavior. Whenever Emily received an angry tongue lashing from Jerry, she would provide a tearful apology, which would mollify Jerry but exacerbate her unhappiness. Her doing so did not solve their ongoing problems.

Emily wanted and needed Jerry to change; she even believed that he could, but he never did. So their habitual pattern, in which Jerry provided the verbal abuse and Emily the apologies, continued for seven years.

Finally, Emily decided that seven years was long enough. She was sick and tired of trying to maintain peace at all costs and made a counseling appointment. In therapy, Emily focused on altering her thoughts and reactions and gave up the idea that Jerry could change. Emily learned and adopted the one-minute rule and the five-minute solution. Her mental fog cleared. She became definitive, and their marriage took a remarkable turn.

Emily: Charging Out of Verbal Abuse with A Plan

Emily was tense at her first session. She was thirty-four years old, tall, and fit. She sat stiffly on the edge of the couch facing me.

In a rush, she said, "I've had a problem for seven years, and I feel desperate. My husband, Jerry, acts like a woman who has monthly periods.

"He begins by putting me down with this kind of talk: 'You should be declared the poster child of dead geraniums. Give it up! Don't be so stupid. You do not have a green thumb.' He was referring to two winters when I tried to save geranium roots and regrow them in the spring.

"As soon as that kind of talk starts, I know we are on either a slow or fast trajectory into what I call his hysterical period. After being mean and nasty for several days, he will be nice for a week or two before going back to being a lunatic.

"He has nice moods where he will talk to me as if I'm an actual person—as he should all the time. But then slowly, day after day, he will start to put me down. He often sneers at me and is sarcastic. I try to ignore that behavior, but whenever he uses his harsh voice, I cannot not pay attention."

She paused and stared at a landscape painting above my head before continuing. "I'm so ridiculous. I hate to even tell you I put up with a man who acts like that. I know I can't change him, but I keep trying to change myself so that he'll stop treating me as if he hates me. What's funny is that when he's in a nice mood, he will say he loves me. Does that make sense?

"His nice talk fools me into thinking that he actually loves me. Can a person who screams at you while practically foaming at the mouth actually love you? Can a person who stands two inches from your face while yelling about how stupid you are actually care on the inside?

"I think constantly about my life, about what to do. Should I leave? Should I stay? I tell him I won't put up with his behavior, but then I do."

After pausing for a breath, Emily said, "My family can barely stand him. They've told me that he is so disrespectful to me he's lucky no one has punched him. I mean, what is wrong with me?

"I stopped working three years ago because Jerry urged me to. He has his own business, so we don't need money. But the problem with not working is having more time to think—I just think and think and think!

"My thoughts constantly dissect our situation. I try to convince myself that things will change if I am nicer or more loving or ignore him or tell him to knock off his abusive behavior, but such thinking gets me nowhere because I struggle to actually say or do what I think. The situations never seem appropriate."

She leaned toward me, keeping her knees together. "I had this same problem in my first marriage, except that my first husband would hit me and be nasty," she said. "I didn't leave him until I was in some state that was probably a nervous breakdown. I don't want to get to that point again. I want you to tell me what to do. You probably won't, though."

"You and I will talk about how to proceed and find solutions to these problems," I said.

Emily sniffled and grabbed a Kleenex.

"Can you remember what you think and feel when your husband begins to rant and rave?" I asked.

"I'll tremble and shake; I'll be furious on the inside. I think things like, 'Why are you so mean to me? I hate you—I wish you were dead!' Some of my thoughts are even nastier, so I don't want to say them out loud."

"Do those thoughts make you feel better?"

"No. I'll be angry and depressed at the same time, but I know I've put myself in this position."

"It has taken you years of growth and development to understand that you are in a vise of your own making—and that realization is a sign of significant growth and development, a major turning point in your life. Congratulations! Your mind is now open and available for other life possibilities. Together, we will explore your thoughts, feelings, and life experiences, and in the meantime, I am going to give you some suggestions to manage these difficult situations with your husband.

Suggestions for Change

"To consciously take control, this is what you must do: think again!" I said. "When you feel caught in circular, upsetting, negative thinking, immediately use the one-minute rule. The second you hear worrisome internal dialogue, stop and take charge of your mind for one minute.

"Try it right now. For one minute, concentrate and repeat a simple phrase like, 'I feel calm.' When your heart is racing because of your husband's words and behavior, order yourself to feel calm and take slow, deep breaths. To do so is important."

Emily sat back and visibly relaxed.

"You should be able to repeat "I feel calm" approximately forty times in one minute. Do you notice how your mind wants to wander? Keep concentrating while you talk to yourself, or your mind will wander away. Catch it—don't let it ramble around or dart into other thoughts. If Jerry's behavior distracts you from the one-minute rule, start again. It is better for you to be focusing on inner calm rather than focusing on his words."

The One-Minute and Five-Minute Rules

With tenacious daily use of the one-minute rule, you will establish a new pathway in your brain, just as consistent running improves your cardiovascular system. For example, if you use the rule consistently with feelings of anxiety, your anxiety will lessen. When you concentrate on the phrase "I feel calm" or similar ones, you will not be thinking other thoughts, so those moments will be free of anxiety. At the same time, you will learn that anxiety is not in control. *You* are in control.

William James, a famous twentieth-century psychologist, once said, "You are what you think all day long." Thinking produces feelings that interpret life's distress or pleasures. Your mind is a magnet that can attract or detract from its own harmonious flow.

Once the one-minute rule is in place, add five minutes of peace; set a timer for a few minutes, and in that time think peacefully. For example, decide that in the car, you will use five minutes to simply think. Check the time, and give yourself time for the five-minute solution. Begin by asking yourself what you want and what actions you can take. Specifically, think about what you want and decide what action, thought, or behavior will place you—not your husband—on the path to resolution.

This is practice thinking. You are not going to act on desires or actions at this moment. You are raising possibilities with yourself. The point of the five-minute solution is to settle down, be serious with yourself and your situation, and think about solutions. Do not fill your mind with distress.

Emily's Issues

Emily's choice in a partner represented her low self-esteem. She married the same personality twice, a personality that could not respect or listen to another person, a personality whose mouth was out of control. If she were to leave her second husband without first developing methods to consciously take charge of herself and to understand what drove her to accept abusive talk and emotional tyranny, her next intimate relationship would be a repeat of the first two.

Instead of focusing on Jerry's verbal abuse, Emily twisted her perceptions into what she thought would placate him. Using this logic, Emily turned her life over to her husband by tiptoeing around him, by putting up with disrespect, by fearing his outbursts, and by experiencing the child inside her crying, whining, and cowering in fear. "Oh, no, what if he yells at me or says nasty things to me? That is awful. I can't stand it when he is mean to me," she would think.

Well, guess what? She was a full participant in exactly what she complained about. Constantly thinking about a relationship does not produce change. Emily's relentless thinking only ground the relationship down with obsessive thoughts. She continuously reiterated to herself that Jerry was mean spirited, and she allowed those habitual thoughts to color her daily life with anxiety and fear. In other words, Emily was a part of the ongoing drama of abuse.

First Steps Toward Solving The Problem
Summary
Whenever Jerry made threats and used intimidation techniques, Emma felt anxious and fearful. To settle such feelings when they arose, Emma must first think about his loud, angry voice and offensive words as the voice of a baby crying at the top of its lungs; the voice is quite annoying but harmless. Second, she needed to avoid looking directly at his menacing face and scary grimaces. Seventy percent of communication lies in facial nuances and body language. Emma was to speak calmly and definitively—these words are meant to sooth her, not Jerry, during his tirade."

I handed her the following list of comments:

- "Yes, I understand how you feel."
- "Yes, I can be unpleasant, distant, crabby, or foolish."

- "Spit it all out. Go on. Tell me more."
- "It must be terrible to be so upset."

Emily laughed to think about talking to Jerry as though she were his psychologist.

Mental Action

"Dedicate yourself to being consciously alert and aware when old anxiety-generating habits sneak into your mind. First, tell yourself, 'Stop it!' Then for one minute, repeat these calming words: 'I manage my reactions. I control myself!'"

Physical Action

"Take charge of your body while you take charge of your mind. Begin by slowly raising your arms while you take a deep breath; then exhale while you drop your arms—repeat all this three times. Next, release and relax your tense stomach muscles.

"Following a tirade, immediately exercise: walk, run in place, lift weights, do jumping jacks, or do push-ups. Do any physical exercise that dispels the tension.

"Slowly but surely fill your mind with the need to focus on clarity in this moment, and pull your thoughts back to calmly control them."

Key Resolutions

"Take charge. Speak your mind without fear, through practicing inner dialogue and through verbalizing calm, appropriate, heart-felt words. You can establish peace within yourself by doing the following:

- Through therapy, gain an understanding of why you need to have your husband hammer your self-esteem while you give in and give up.
- Shift your focus from your distress to your goals.
- Ask no more questions about why Jerry acts as he does. Jerry will not change. Cement in your mind that Jerry's words and behavior are written in stone. Figure out your why.
- Plan a future with Jerry or without him. If your future is with Jerry, learn how to accommodate yourself to his behavior."

Therapy Wrap-Up

Six months into her therapy, Emily decided to divorce Jerry. Jerry, much to Emily's surprise, screamed, cried, and told Emily, "I cannot live without you. I love you. Please, don't leave me—I'm begging you."

Emily was shocked by his declaration of love but did not drop the divorce. Instead, she asked her attorney to put the divorce on hold to determine if there was any depth to Jerry's words.

Was Jerry reacting with loving words to stay in control, or was there actually hope for the marriage? Emily needed time. As much as Jerry tried to manage himself, his old behavior kept inserting itself into the relationship. Emily wavered back and forth, but she realized she could never be herself with a critical, angry person. Divorce was the answer.

Through therapy and conscious attention to thoughts and feelings, Emily discovered that she no longer cared whether Jerry really loved her or not. Fortunately, Emily's mind had not turned to brain-tortured mush, which usually happens after a person's self-esteem is trampled daily and the recipient is incapable of warding off the blows.

CHAPTER 4
Tit-For-Tat Anger

The mind is pristine. You live in your mind, where your feelings, thoughts, and imagination belong to you alone. Watching your face, body movements, and tone of voice may provide clues, but no one can read your mind or understand your emotional state unless you reveal your mental activity. A state-of-the-art mind-imaging machine (fMRI) can reveal that you are having thoughts and feelings, but the fMRI printout displays only brain activity—not content.

When you interpret your partner's words and behavior as loving and in your best interest, your brain waves are calm and orderly. On the other hand, if you imagine or experience your partner as upset and angry, your brain waves spike and jump, sending displeasure, anger, and fear spiraling through your system.

Anger Prisoners
Amy and Jason were experts at expressing their feelings through body language and facial expressions. They were mind readers as well, responding to words spoken and imagined; their imagined interpretations were pessimistic and antagonistic.

This couple's stated goal for relationship therapy was to reestablish their happiness, love, and respect for one another. When their therapy began anger was the solution to their problems—anger that wiped out their love and established a vigilant, ambush-ready mind-set. Constantly fearing that their egos would be squashed, they continually blamed each other for the angry tension that always developed. They had worked on their unhappy marriage with me in a previous therapy sessions and had altered their habitual sharp words and behavior; however, rage crept back slowly and insidiously, corroding their relationship once again.

In my office for a counseling session, Jason, who was forty years old, slumped on my office couch like a sulky child. Amy, Jason's thirty-nine-year-old wife, made a face while she pushed her hair back. They were body experts at conveying their exasperation and ill temper through meaningful looks and subtle movements.

Jason

Jason was chunky and had curly dark hair. His height was average. His clothes looked rumpled, as if he had thrown them on while running out the door. Professionally, he taught seminars. He was a speaker who toured the country with an entourage of energized, up-beat people; he advised companies and individuals about how to keep their life on positive, productive paths.

When Jason was in concrete work settings or with strangers, he focused his intensely passionate feelings in a positive manner. He was always in charge of himself in those settings. In the intimacy of his family, he was always on edge, loud, and angry.

Jason reported that Amy's constant talk drove him crazy. After seventeen years of marriage, he still responded to her chatter with irritation. In his mind, Amy was responsible for their bickering and arguments.

Amy

Amy was about five feet five inches tall and had blond hair. She was dressed in jeans and had long manicured nails. She sat stiffly on the couch, her hands moving quickly whenever she talked. Amy ran a flower-arranging business, but she spent most of her time at home, where she was kept busy caring for their twelve-year-old daughter and fifteen-year-old son. She said she was unhappy in the marriage because "Jason never listens to me. He always acts as if he's mad at me and the children."

Therapy

Opposition in all life's arenas was their passion and pleasure. Parenting, decorating their home, spending money, and going to their cottage were opportunities to argue. The emotional chaos generated by their heated disagreements set the tone in their home.

Amy said, "Our problem this time began when Jason refused to stop fighting in front of the children."

"For Pete's sake, Amy," said Jason, cutting in, "the kids can hear us wherever we are. The way you screech, everyone within a five-mile radius knows every one of our problems."

"Your criticizing each other is digging your hole of unhappiness deeper and is not acceptable in my office," I said. "I can only listen to one person at a time. We are here to solve problems, not to fight. Let's allow each person his or her own reality without negative comments."

Jason sat back semirelaxed.

After giving Jason a stern look, Amy continued and said, "Anyway, as I was saying, our fighting is vicious and upsets me so much that we do not have good times. We used to at least have good times between the bad times. For months, everything has been nothing but bad times.

"I feel lonely, angry, and frustrated; I don't feel like we're companions. I've tried everything to win Jason over, to no avail. Jason doesn't like me—that's the bottom line."

Jason was silent.

I waited and then said, "Jason, it sounds as if Amy has been miserable. How are you feeling?"

"How do you think I feel?" he said.

"Unless you tell me, I won't know."

Jason conceded. "Well, there is nothing I can do to please Amy. She is always comparing us to other people. Our house is always in the process of being painted or wallpapered or something similar because Amy is never satisfied. Most of all, she is not satisfied with me. Nothing ever gets done, solved, or finished.

"If I say white, she says black. If I try to suggest a solution, she says I'm controlling or bossing her. On my way home from the office, I'm always irritable because I anticipate problems."

It seemed as if Jason was always ready for battle whenever he walked through the door to their home. Whatever messages Amy wanted to convey were lost when Jason interpreted her expressions as reprimands. He would then respond viscerally. His system would flood with emotions, and around they would go.

In general, active minds enhance lives and marriages. In Amy and Jason's case, their active minds were detonating devices, watching and waiting for the first wrong step. Their minds were constantly warring in a marital minefield, and the first words were the equivalent of lobbed grenades.

Train the Brain

In *The Mind and the Brain*, Jeffrey M. Schwartz states that "an invisible machine located in the brain called the mind runs your life via your thoughts. You are the mechanic in charge of the engine that activates your brain. Your brain is the engine. Attention and direction are the fuel. Your mind is the engineer."

When anger is the relationship issue, the engineer needs immediate solutions to drop into the brain's control panel to stop hostile feelings. Either a method to manage the natural, reflexive response of being startled in the face of anger needs to be implemented, or the thoughts of rage that are ramping up in response to the hostility need to be dampened.

One method is to depersonalize yourself by imagining you are watching and listening to a ridiculous drama totally unrelated to you or to exit quickly when you notice negative tones, words of anger, aggressive looks, or belligerent body language. Another solution is to catch and stop your repeated thought patterns that whip up anger as a response.

Thoughts of altering and retraining habitual thoughts may seem simple, but it is important to know at the outset that sticking with the plan is difficult because there is a natural tendency to continuously cycle anger issues rather than focus on anger solutions.

Conscious awareness is necessary to catch and block even the beginning of angry words and feelings. Combat and resist old reactive habits, and do not cave in. Constantly remind yourself from the moment you wake up that you are calm and in control. As soon as you catch a negative thought, stop it and change it. Replace it immediately with your goal.

The easy path is to fall back into habitual negative thoughts and feelings. Be patient with yourself because it takes at least six months to establish new thinking.

Take Action

You have a choice: either leave the relationship or change your thinking. If you choose to live with an angry person but desire happiness, the perspective choice is to depersonalize. To do so, keep in mind that anger has nothing to do with you, even though the harsh talk and feelings are aimed at you. The problem is within your partner.

Do not make defensive comments or argue. When you do you immerse yourself in the other person's game, you are turning their problem into your own.

I posed a specific question to Amy and Jason. "What do you want?" I asked.

Jason said, "Peace." He did not look peaceful.

Sitting on the edge of her seat and twisting her wedding ring, Amy said, "I want Jason to control his anger."

Establishing peace and learning to control anger are desirable and achievable goals. Peace is not anger's companion. Peace begins with the acknowledgment that you have chosen to live an emotionally chaotic existence thus far and that your relationship with your partner is a volcano that can erupt in a heartbeat. You are on an automatic snap and bark approach to each other, which guarantees that you will disturb each other.

Either of you can alter these disturbing rituals, but it would be ideal if both of you tried to do so. When partnership satisfaction depends upon the other person's changing, you become powerless. Stop pointing your finger at your partner. This is your life.

To an angry person, venting anger feels good because tension is released, but it does not end there—anger begets anger. The more aggressive you feel, the more apt you become to act your anger out and keep it up; in the meantime, you only stimulate your partner's hostility.

Expressing anger frequently decreases tolerance and flexibility. It sets up a war zone of vigilance and fear. Instead of communicating to solve problems, your giving into anger erects defensive barriers that make it difficult to switch from vigilance to trust or from ranting and raving to appreciation and love.

Therapy Discussion

"At this point, your ability to solve problems in your relationship has disappeared," I said. "Angry thought patterns and aggressive behavior have calcified. You are opponents instead of allies. Is that right?"

They agreed but give each other a look.

"At the same time, you both desperately seem to want a peaceful relationship. If you choose not to change, admit that you love being contentious, nasty, and mean.

"You two are perfect candidates for change. Both of you can multitask, and you both are smart and persistent—the latter quality is evidenced by your daily disagreements.

"Let's set up new persistence tasks of peace and control. You will switch from engaging in agitated, angry confrontations to continuously thinking of calm self-management.

"I cannot stress this enough. If you wanted to build a muscle and began to lift weights, would you expect muscle mass in a month? Of course not.

"You will be changing neurological patterns of discontent and aggression that have been in place for years. It takes time and patience to train your brain. Both of you have the mental capacity and the ability to establish new habits while carrying on normal activities and focusing on your goals.

"That being said, the doing—that is, the taking charge of yourself—is the difficulty. Changing an angry habit of mind means being aware of thoughts and feelings that trigger anger.

"Here is a simple example: you monitor your mind when you are listening to someone; while you listen, you think about potential responses. In other words, you are capable of experiencing a two-track mind—a mind monitor."

The Plan

"If you are serious about improving your relationship, time and effort are required, and a long-term plan is needed to obliterate old reactions and institute new ideas. Say things like this to yourself: 'I can't wait to begin, to change, and to take charge of my brain.' In other words, whip up enthusiasm; you are in the process of feeling good, even great, about your relationship.

"Beginning today, plan on two to four months (and forever afterward) of uttering calming mantras daily to yourself and to your spouse."

I gave them the following list to study:

- Many times a day, repeat the following to yourself: "I am calm, I feel calm, and I act calm" (speak slowly, take five seconds).
- Relax. Take deep breaths.
- Respond positively when your partner speaks. Say that his or her ideas are great, even if you have other ideas that you think are better.
- Empathize. Tell you partner that you realize he or she is upset, but say *nothing* else.
- Do *not* convey feelings giving snotty looks, rolling your eyes, shaking your head, or raising your voice.
- Do *not* respond by saying something like "you have to do what the therapist said" or "that's not what you are supposed to say" or "don't you have a mind of your own?"

To Amy

"You know you cannot control another person, right?" I said.

Amy agreed.

"Your job is to manage yourself, which you have not been doing. Stick with one thought. For example, when Jason is angry, even though you may feel the surge of old agitated thoughts and feelings, calm yourself. To respond, simply say that you understand."

Amy showed her agitation. "Well, I shouldn't have to manage myself because he is out of control."

"Right. I agree. You should not, but at the same time, you want to solve this problem. And isn't it true that you have become an out-of-control person too?"

"Sometimes."

"Imagine that he will be an angry person forever and that you have to live with him. What do you do? Either you can add decibels to each screaming match, which will upset and disturb you, or you can view him as a two-year-old. His anger has nothing to do with you.

"If he verbalizes an issue with you, remember that when you become defensive, you will exacerbate the problem. Your defenses consist in you explaining yourself—not in listening to his words, thinking destructive thoughts in the face of his anger, or shouting back.

"Stop it! Listen to him. Actually pay attention to what he is saying. Acknowledge whatever he says as though he were telling you a story. Remind yourself that he has a right to his opinion but that it has nothing to do with you, even though he might use your name repeatedly. Or think other calming thoughts.

"Take charge of the situation by taking charge of yourself. Before his anger surfaces, before any confrontation, rehearse the following response: 'That's interesting. I feel that way sometimes. I know it is difficult, but tell me more.'

"Do not act on the forceful thoughts that prompt your defenses. Such thoughts may resemble the following: 'You are wrong. I did not do that. You do that too.' These are old habits, automatic words that do not promote peace.

To Jason
"Break the cycle of attacking your partner. *You* stop. If you desire peace, you know it is up to you to take charge of yourself. Anger begets anger.

"You feel like shouting and yelling. So what? Sometimes you feel like yelling at a customer. Do you? No. You control yourself.

"The idea that you have to respond with anger is a habit that relieves tension momentarily, but after lashing out, you actually do not feel better, nor are the problems between you and your wife resolved after you do so."

"When a hint of anger begins, immediately *stop*. Expect anger to surface. Do not under any circumstances express your anger. Go upstairs, go downstairs and run on your treadmill, or go outside—do anything that moves you away from the anger scene.

"Respect Amy's point of view and respond by simply acknowledging that her idea has been heard. It is possible for you to say to Amy that you understand her. Do not jump in with another idea or solution, even if you think it is positive. If you feel you have to respond tit for tat, go to your computer and write a story about the situation and what you want and expect from yourself.

To Amy and Jason

"You are not the judge and jury of your partner's thoughts and feelings. Nuances in the face and body language send messages; conscious control of negative facial and body language is critical."

I gave them the following list of to-do items:

- Stop impulsive reactions, including the manipulative use of tone.
- Stay focused on what you want in the marriage, not on what you do not like or do not want.
- To get what you want, think about solving your own problems, not your partner's.
- You are responsible for your happiness. You are not a victim.

- Stay neutral: do not sneer, contort your faces, swivel your heads, roll your eyes, and so forth.
- Remember that you can terminate the marriage at any time, but you have chosen not to.

"If you cannot remember calming thoughts for yourselves, remember that war zones are unhealthy for children. Modeling methods to solve problems rather than screaming like a nine-year-old child (most nine-year-olds are smarter than that) should be foremost in your minds."

Amy and Jason struggled once again to make changes, working to eliminate anger and nasty confrontations; their daily challenge was to show love and affection. After a year of weekly counseling, they needed monthly marriage-counseling sessions to reestablish and remind themselves of their marital goals. They have not separated or divorced each other, and they still seem to have a powerful need to be together.

CHAPTER 5
Specific Repetitive Anger

The essence of June's problem was specific disrespectful behavior acted out over forty years without a solution; like an ongoing infection, it would flare up and tear and rip at her otherwise happy marital relationship. Rather than focus on solutions, June used anger to deflect her problems with her husband; essentially, she had been angry at his disrespectful and, in her eyes, abusive behavior for years. She reported that she would not continue to participate in their relationship, but she was stymied and thought divorce might be the only answer.

Ongoing negative feelings, no matter the length of a marriage, need to be acknowledged as problems and solved. To entertain upsetting thought patterns and feelings for forty years, as June did, is unhealthy for the mind, body, and relationships.

June's and Hal's Specific Angry Thoughts and Feelings
Although I had difficulty understanding June's entire message on my voice mail, I did understand her desperation.

"Please, please, help me," she said.

Since she indicated that she lived at least an hour and a half away from my office, I called her back, intent on giving her both a referral and a number of a crisis center to call immediately. When I reached June, she insisted that she must see only me because her trusted friend had referred her. We set up an appointment early the next day.

Given her frantic message, I was not sure of what to expect that morning, but I was surprised. June was seventy-five, Korean, dignified, and elegant. Her skin was clear and unwrinkled. She dressed stylishly, and from the back, she appeared to be a young woman.

June was miserable as a result of ongoing issues in her marriage. Looking into my eyes, she said, "My husband, Hal, is seventy-two, and he retired seven years ago. He has not respected me from day one, fifty years ago, the day we met in Korea."

June owned a tailoring shop on a US Air Force base in Korea, and when Hal came in to pick up shirts, it was love at first sight. Hal left Korea a year later and vowed he would be back to marry June. Hal kept his word.

When June and Hal went to the commander of the base for authorization to marry, necessary in the military overseas, the commander did not hassle them. (According to June, others seeking the authorization to marry were often hassled at the time.) Instead, the commander asked Hal, "Where did you find this lovely woman?"

It was clear to me that the commander's words of respect and admiration were so powerful they reverberated through the years, but that memory contrasted sharply with June's persistent life-long turmoil she had experienced whenever her husband "disrespected" her.

Hal's behavior at home had been the glue in their relationship. In a measured, quiet voice, June said, "At home, Hal tells me he loves me and is very nice to me, but if we are out, he acts like I am not around. The last straw was our grandson's wedding on Saturday. He ignored me and stared at other women, making eye contact and then talking flirta-tiously—even at his age!

"When we eat out, he spends his time ogling other women. He is so obvious that I find that behavior disgusting. I am so upset and angry I can't eat. When I talk to him about his behavior or anything else that bothers me, he gets angry and says something like, 'You don't under-stand' or 'You don't get it.' That is his way of shutting me up."

While she told her story, June began to cry and then quickly apolo-gized for her tears. I told June my office would not know what to do without emotions. I asked June if her husband embarrassed her.

"Yes," she said, whispering, tiny tears spilling from her eyes. "Yes, yes."

The Solution

"Live in this moment," I said. "If you are feeling distressed, think! Ask yourself why you are distressed. These feelings are real. Emotions are to be examined intellectually and taken seriously. Try to determine whether your feelings are habit driven and historical. Ask yourself what your feel-ings are and what you can do about them.

"Take charge of your feelings and thoughts; eliminate not only the habitual dialogue with yourself but also the same-old discussions with your husband that do nothing but make you upset and angry. Use the one-minute rule to calm and alter thoughts. Then decide on a plan that implements different words and behavior.

"June, take charge of your restaurant behavior—not Hal's. Your mes-sages to your husband have never worked or made a difference. Why would saying them again effect change?"

The next time they made plans to dine out, June was to inform Hal nicely but firmly that she liked being with him and liked to eat out with him but that she felt uncomfortable when he stared and talked to other women. She was to say that behavior was unacceptable.

If Hal were to say that he did not look longingly at other women or to state that June was imagining things, she was to reply that she was aware of his thinking. However, that was not how she thought or felt. Then she was to do either of two things: tell Hal that their dinner plans were off or decide at the restaurant whether she could tolerate his behavior.

June was prepared with a plan. She would drive her own car to the restaurant, or if she was uncomfortable driving alone and his behavior persisted, she would get a taxi. If she was unable to follow through, she let Hal know that she had no backbone and was all talk.

Thoughts Direct Behavior

Hal's refusal to acknowledge his behavior had stymied June, and she failed to realize that when her husband did not respond to whatever she was saying or altogether denied her sense of reality, her words became meaningless. Rather than continually react to Hal, June was to be the actor.

Action carries a risk, however. It is important to assess what is the worst that can happen. In June and Hal's case, he will not like the talk, he will get angry, he will refuse to go out to eat, or he will change his behavior. It was very important for June to recognize potential consequences and to decide whether she was up to each of these possibilities before she talked to Hal.

June shocked me. Immediately after the first therapy session, June told me that she had taken charge of herself. "I quit acting like a baby," she said.

June said the change was a miracle. Hal did not know what to make of the difference in June. He responded positively. His disrespectful restaurant behavior collapsed. I told June that one success did not mean back to business as usual; she needed to be vigilant and continue her staunch attitude. She was not to put up with any disrespectful behavior.

June's experience in therapy is an example of thought alteration that has the potential to transform a partnership so completely, so radically, and so marvelously that after only a few short months, a relationship founded on positivity can emerge.

CHAPTER 6
Repetitive Anger

Repetitive anger is intense and meant to punish, educate, and control a partner's behavior. Propelled by inner dialogue that is tense and agitated, angry people feed on anger's emotional exhilaration and excitement, acting out their rage and repeating the same angry mantras.

Acted-out anger serves another purpose: it is an elevator maneuver used in an attempt to raise the angry person's self-esteem and, at the same time, humiliate and crush the recipient's self-esteem.

In the mind of the raging individual, the person attacked is properly punished and educated in regard to the imagined bad behavior. Wrong! In fact, the education that occurs is a feeling of being demeaned and criticized without reason; the recipients are often frightened by the fury of the attack and experience an overwhelming desire to get away.

Individuals who are addicted to expressing intense anger as a way to control relationships have no regard for their partners. When a partner reacts by turning off and turning away instead of being deeply hurt, the fury intensifies. This sick cycle may go on for years.

Melanie

Melanie's marriage cycle lasted eight years, which is about the average length of time it takes for partners to grasp the truth that nothing about the other person is going to change, regardless of castigating anger, silence, or thoughtful explanations of hurt feelings.

Melanie, a thirty-two-year-old librarian, reported that she was addicted to regular outbursts of rage, in which she often demanded that her husband behave differently. The fact that he ignored her never calmed her anger.

After years of screaming fits, Melanie called for counseling. In therapy, Melanie stated that she was once a lighthearted career woman in love with a wonderful man, but the reality of her husband's personality had turned her sweet love into a sour, angry relationship disappointment.

Therapy

Melanie left a message on my office phone. When I returned her call, she said, "I'd like to make an appointment as quickly as possible. I've had your name for over a year and just put off calling, but when I heard the garage door go up today, I ran and stood waiting, ready to kill my husband—and I'm not kidding. I was so infuriated that he was lucky I didn't have a gun!"

That sounded like an emergency to me, but Melanie's "I need an appointment as quickly as possible" turned into a three-week turnaround. She had so many stumbling blocks—two small children, a job, other appointments, and having to deal with her husband—that several calls were required to cement a date and time to meet.

Melanie greeted me, looked my office over, and chose a comfortable seat. Her calm behavior contrasted sharply with her dramatic "I'm going to kill my husband" phone call.

After answering intake questions, Melanie asked if I would be interested in her list of three major problems. I said that I was.

Melanie read aloud from a notebook. "First, I feel empty. I do nothing for myself, which I think is okay because I am a mom. Second, I don't like my husband—sometimes I hate him. Third, I'm sick about my indecision, and I don't know what to do to change myself."

She put the notebook down. "I used to love being the mom and housewife. Now, I find making simple appointments to be a harrowing experience." Anxiously twisting her Kleenex, she said, "Managing the coordination and logistics of calling, rearranging, rushing, and suspecting I've forgotten something is exhausting.

"In the morning, I'm okay, probably because I'm like a cat chasing its tail—there's no time to think. Then as the day wears on, I feel the weight of my life pulling me down. I feel heavy, as though I'm walking through water, and I dread the whole Mike thing."

"The Mike thing?" I asked.

"Well, every afternoon at about five, my husband, Mike, calls and says he's on his way home—but he's not. Then he calls again to say he got held up." She then mumbled something I could not hear.

"What?"

"I despise him!"

"Why do you despise him?"

"I can't talk about that now—I have to tell you what happens first."

"When the garage door finally goes up, it is about half past eight or nine o'clock, which means that I've fed, bathed, and put the kids to bed and he's going to come in like a hero, run upstairs, and get them all worked up again.

"I always tell him the kids had been waiting for him and asking me when he would be home. I always point out that he waits until they're in bed to kiss them and say good night.

"He does this almost every night, and I'm always upset about it! I've talked to him constantly about his behavior but to no avail. I know I'm not an idiot, but I sure am acting like one. What is wrong with me?"

"What do you think is wrong with you?" I asked.

Melanie hesitated and then said, "I don't love Michael; he's an impediment. I need to get rid of him, but I'm stymied. If my kids were not my main concern, I'd be out of there. Michael would be history."

She rearranged herself and sat up straight before continuing. "Brandon, our four-year-old son, is on the autistic spectrum. I don't have to tell you what that involves. Brandon sops up my love and energy, and that's fine, except I feel guilty because it cheats my seven-year-old of attention. Where my husband could pick up the slack, he doesn't. He can't seem to focus on the kids, and I can't do it all."

She squirmed on the couch before getting to the next part. "Because of my hours of toting Brandon to a variety of doctors and therapies, because of my spending so much time working with him at home, he is doing quite well. And, trust me, I'm not upset about the time I spend with my Brandon.

"I feel like a single parent. I used to be frustrated; now my anger is nonstop. It oozes out of my pores! Here's a tiny example: Michael came home late one night. I did not want to say anything, but I could'nt help it." She waved her arms. "I yelled, 'What is wrong with you? Are you an idiot?' I could not seem to stop myself. I then screamed, 'Get out of here. You are useless. You don't care about any of us, you moron.'

"In general, I want to slap and hit him, but usually I restrain myself. So who's the idiot? I think it's me."

Visibly shaken, Melanie slumped in her chair, tears welling at her lids.

"Michael is so distasteful to me that I refuse to have sex or anything physical with him, even kissing. This has been going on for two years now. You would think that without sex, Mike would say, 'I'm out of here.' But, no, he keeps bugging me for sex, trying to be nicer—when he's home that is!

"Truthfully, I want a divorce, but I'm tormented by the idea of breaking up the family and causing my children even more pain."

I summarized what Melanie had shared to be sure that I understood her; then I tried to help her step back and assess her situation. "Your expectations for your husband are unmet, and you are chronically disappointed," I said. "Your husband's behavior, although not to your liking, is predictable. He always calls. He is always late. He always wants sex. He never grasps your needs. He is not empathic or supportive of you.

"Have you considered the possibility that your husband and son may share some of the same autistic traits? Both have difficulty reading the emotions of others; both have limited social skills.

"If your husband is not on the autistic spectrum, he has nevertheless amply demonstrated his unwillingness and inability to relate closely to either you or your children. Since it is not within your power to change your husband's behavior, especially when he shows no inclination to recognize your concerns, you are caught in a bind.

"Instead of facing the reality of who Michael is—a husband who is not responsive to your requests and expectations—you have become an angry person, as well as habit driven, depressed, and frustrated. Is that how you feel?"

"Yes."

"Then the following ideas may help you change your perspective: First, you have the ability to be in charge of your own behavior, thoughts, and feelings, but you cannot change those of an unwilling or incapable other. Second, the victims are your children, who are being battered emotionally without the power to effectively resist or change your family's dynamics. Third, by blaming your husband, you continue the myth that he is susceptible to and capable of acting as you wish, despite evidence to the contrary."

Crying and nodding, she said, "Yes, I know." She thought for a while.

Realizing the effect her behavior had on her children, Melanie said, "This is cute but so sad: on Sunday, when he saw his father mowing the lawn, Brad said, 'Mom, your husband is working hard.' He was trying to cheer me up.

"It made me laugh but talk about guilt! Brad, in his own way, is trying to help me appreciate his dad. If I ever wondered whether the kids were being affected by my relationship with Mike, I now know they are. The answer is they know I'm upset with him and their awareness of the fact is affecting them.

"I try not to fight in front of the kids. You know how that goes. I talk through clenched teeth, but I'm sure they always hear us arguing."

Background

When we met again, I asked Melanie to tell me about her relationship with her parents.

"We have a good relationship; I talk to my dad every morning on my way to the library. We talk about my work or child issues, but he has made it clear he does not want to hear about my marriage.

"My father has a loud voice that scared me when I was little. He used to get really mad and blow up—not at me but at whatever he didn't like at the time. My dad is all about getting things done and getting them done right.

"He and I took charge of my mother, my little sister, and everything around the house because my mother could not organize her way out of a closet. She was hopelessly inefficient."

"You and your father were your mother's caretaker?"

Melanie launched into an explanation in a roundabout way. "My sister thinks he's critical and difficult; I say he has high expectations. My father is a successful attorney with several partners and at least twenty employees. I'm like my dad: I have high expectations, and I enjoy being organized.

"Even though I have a great relationship with my father, for some reason I feel closer to my mother. My mother is ditsy and sweet but frustrating. She never remembers conversations, and if she says she will do something, sometimes it gets done and sometimes it does'nt. But she has an extraordinary IQ and can do any crossword in a minute."

"In what way do you feel close to her? It sounds as if she's not available and doesn't show any interest in you."

"I guess you could say that, but she's not interested in my father or sister either, so I don't take it personally. For example, when I was a teenager, there were no curfews. My mother never asked where I was going. I announced where I would be. In fact, I told my friends I had to be home at a certain time because they all had limits and I wanted to be like them.

"My father belonged to so many professional organizations that after dinner, he would lay out instructions for us and then disappear." She paused to slip off her shoes and move her legs under her skirt. "I did make sure I got home before my dad, so maybe that was my curfew.

"I think I'm close to my mom because she's a loving, huggy person and says she loves me. As an adult, I see how difficult her life was and is."

"In what way is your mother's life difficult?"

"Well, as you can tell, my dad is the king. When he tells us to jump, we do so quickly, or there will be hell to pay."

Assessment

"You portray your mother as someone who is a nonparticipant in the family, but you know she is motherly and quick to share her hugs and love. Your mother might be trying to fly under the radar of your father's criticism. A person who is criticized often and can never seem to do anything right may choose to do nothing at all.

"Your husband is similar to your mother. He is distant, unorganized, and unobservant, and he lives in his own world. But unlike your mother, he focuses on what he wants—sex.

"Having to live with a loud, angry father, you chose to side with him, acting in accordance to his need for perfection, and rather than model your behavior after your helpless mother, you identified with your father—the aggressor. Like your father, you are angry and demanding. You have high expectations, but your husband ignores you, as your mother does."

Results of Modeling

"You have learned to be tenacious and direct, which is excellent, but using your father's style to alter your husband's behavior does not work."

"I know. How stupid!"

"It's not stupid. Parents, whether good or bad, are our relationship models. As you grew up, you saw that your father's methods worked for him."

"I've always been proud to be like my father, but I see that I need to temper my temper," she said, laughing. "It's such a relief to laugh because my life seems so serious. I guess that if, as you say, I am responsible for my life, I've turned it into a nightmare for myself. Maybe I need to lighten up."

"If you lightened up, what would happen?" I asked.

"I think I would be able to slow down my mad thoughts and stop some of my ranting. I do have it in my mind to change. It just hasn't happened."

"You dwell on the idea that your husband is unavailable; you feel that you are on your own, and that makes you angry. At the same time, you don't want him around—that seems paradoxical."

Melanie responded quietly and slowly. "This sounds terrible: he is a successful business man, which influences me, but I don't want him near me. I just want him to be a good father and to pay attention to my children."

"Let me share some thoughts that should be helpful. Just for a moment, accept your husband for what he is. The idea that he will be different is not founded on reality; rather, the idea is based on imaginative thoughts of how he should be. Replaying the tape in your mind of anger and displeasure toward your husband is an infection spreading through your system and depleting your energy.

"You chose Michael because he has positive attributes. Make a conscious choice to replace angry, negative, and mean thoughts with benign and positive ones. These conscious thoughts are not about your husband; they are meant to restore balance within yourself."

How to Alter Habitual Thinking

"Thoughts are things. You are not a thing; therefore, you are not your thoughts. The brain continuously churns out little snippets of random information and ideas, approximately sixty thousand bits each day. A thought that comes to mind will mean nothing unless you give it significance.

"*Mindfulness* is moment-to-moment awareness of your thoughts, emotions, and sensations. It will provide you with what is called the "observing ego," a perspective that will allow you to be an observer and decider as opposed to an automatic responder.

"Mindfulness will allow you to dismiss a thought or focus on it, so you will not have to tell yourself that each thought is important simply because it came to mind. For example, your brain throws a nagging, troubling thought into your mind: your daughter may be on drugs. If you are mindful, you will not keep circling around, turning the thought into a calamity; you either dismiss the thought or make a decision to take action.

"Some thoughts repeatedly float into our minds, especially if they are attached to an emotion, such as anger. Does an angry thought indicate the thought or feeling is useful or positive or should be acted upon? No. It may be random, or it may be a habitual thinking habit.

"To be a mindful person is not easy because mindfulness requires focus. We are lazy. It is easier to stick with ingrained habits of the mind that go nowhere than to make our minds' mind."

Summary for Change

I gave Melanie the following list:

- You must determine the future of your relationship. Stop repetitive angry thoughts. Constant angry thoughts are like ingesting a little poison every day. They sicken you. Nothing is solved.
- Peace of mind is first and foremost. Your agitated state is a deterrent to a solution.
- Accept what is.
- As you drop off to sleep at night, calm your mind, do not allow your troubles to infiltrate, overtake, and impair your sleep. Concentrate on peace.
- In the morning and before your children are up, sit down for five minutes and write out positive mind goals for the day. No matter how busy you are, you can carve out five minutes.
- Focus totally in those five minutes (be mindful).

Melanie wanted these ideas e-mailed to her so that she could concentrate and repeat them. When Melanie came in for her next session, she brought in another five sentences describing her feelings toward her husband:

1. Michael abandoned me when I desperately needed him.
2. I used to feel anger and disgust; now I look at him and feel nothing.
3. He denied my pain about Brandon's autism.
4. He did not participate in the many appointments and caretaking necessary for Brandon's growth and development.
5. I feel as if I have been emotionally divorced for at least two years.

Therapy Results

After a long process of inner and outer discovery, Melanie was unable or would not allow herself to think positively about her husband.

"I'm done with him," she said. "My anger is gone. Therapy has helped me realize I do not respect Mike. I cannot live with a person who says one thing and does another. Really, his personality is offensive to me. I am unable to think about Mike's positive attributes. I'm over being angry, though; I have no more fury and wild feelings. When I look at him or think about him, I feel as if I'm viewing a stranger."

Melanie's Solution

Melanie made the decision to divorce and chose to continue therapy while in the divorce process to help herself and her children move through the rough, emotional separation in the best-possible manner. She delved into divorce information, wanting to understand what to expect in every area, child custody, finances, time lines, and the cost of divorce. She probed all the choices and possible consequences. Her rationale was familiar. The intact family was ideal, but the hostility and rancor between her and her husband was not good for the children or herself.

CHAPTER 7
Anger Turned Against the Self

Thinking and feeling are intertwined. Most of us use both emotion and intellect to understand people and the world, but there are individuals who base their behaviors and understanding of life either on their intellect or on their emotions.

Intellectually focused individuals ignore feelings for a variety of reasons. For example, if an individual is born with few emotional brain conduits (an area in the brain called the amygdala), that individual cannot be empathic because their brain is already compromised. Or intellectually focused individuals may have learned in their original families that emotions are a sign of weakness. It may be these individuals were traumatized and have an unconscious fear of being emotionally vulnerable.

An emotional person reacts primarily to feelings; they are overwhelmed by feelings, and the intellect usually takes a back seat.

Susan is an emotional person whose judgment was impaired. Her intellect could not dislodge emotions that were clouding her mind.

Susan

Susan was fifty years old when she came to me for therapy. She was pale, tall, and lanky, and she wore high heels and a dress at our first session.

Her problem was that she loathed herself and had chosen a man who used and abused her.

"I know my situation is abusive, but I am incapable of leaving. Inside, I know I'm not worth anything. I've done things in my life that I'm ashamed of, and when Steve says, 'You are a piece of shit,' he's right. I am. At work, I'm okay. In fact, I've been promoted regularly and make an excellent salary, but those smarts don't translate to my relationship."

Susan had lived with Steve for sixteen years. He was an angry fifty-four-year-old and always seemed to be acting out. He was emotionally abusive, and sometimes that abuse turned physical. The final insult, she said, was that after all she had put up with, Steve was having an affair with his associate and flaunting it.

Susan lived in fear, like every abused person, and although she intellectually realized the situation was not in her best interest, her emotions prevented her from telling him good-bye.

She squeezed her hands together and continued to belittle herself. "When I get so angry and disgusted that I actually assert myself, he backs down and feels sorry. He loves me. Then, believe it or not, I feel good.

"I can't constantly be mad at him; it upsets me too much. Steve ridicules me and denies what he has just said, and then he speaks nicely and I melt. I'm a fool and I know it." She grinned, but her grin implied that she did not actually feel like a fool.

The criteria for Susan's life were her feelings. Either she was filled with anguish and anger inspired by his abuse, or she was giddy with Steve's expressed love for her.

Susan's Life

Susan was living a lie. If a stranger looked in from the outside, her life would appear perfect. Susan had an administrative position with a large corporation. Her husband was tall, handsome, and well spoken, and he had a career in a prestigious business. They owned a home on a lake, as well as boats, cars, and even a plane.

Susan thought others viewed her as a confident professional with a good marriage. The people who knew them were not stupid; they heard his tone and saw the way he put her down. Steve spoke to Susan as if she were a demented servant, and she allowed him to chastise, deride, and scold her. Her rationale was "I don't have it in me to keep arguing. I'm angry and disgusted with myself most of the time."

Nevertheless, Susan bravely took two steps, revealing her real life in therapy and opening up to friends. Talking about her situation was the first step, but she could not take the next action-oriented step to behave differently or seek a separation or both. Instead, she raged to herself about her lack of resolve, fell back into her emotionally chaotic life, and soon left counseling.

Susan's background put her on a path that ended in low or no self-worth and gave her a historical fear of poverty.

History

Life for Susan had not always been a financial breeze. Her young life was spent in poverty. Her father could not hold onto a job, and her mother was pregnant and sick most of Susan's life. She was the oldest of seven children; the last sibling was born when she was ten.

Susan was never a child. From the time Susan could toddle around, her mother needed help. Susan filled in as the surrogate mom. When she was only two years old, she would bring diapers to her mother; when she was four, she would rock babies to sleep and straighten up the house. There was never a time to go out and play—she always had work to do.

Besides being the housekeeper and babysitter—both of which should have brought her praise—Susan was the tall, freckled, and skinny target of the family's jokes. Her salvation was school. Although she was the poorest kid with unkempt hair and wore the same clothes every day, she knew she was the smartest kid in class, and her teachers loved her— she could be called on to answer any question.

Susan's father was brutal and verbally abusive, and he had a physical mean streak. She remembered that he criticized her from the time he walked through the door (if he actually bothered to come home) to the time she went to bed. Her mother was too tired and busy to protect her. If her mother did say anything, she would become the fodder for sarcasm, a slap, or something worse. Much later, Susan discovered that her father had a girlfriend and two more children.

Susan missed her appointments without calling. My calls to her were not returned.

Return To Therapy

Six months later, Susan returned to therapy, drowning in fear. She knew more than she had ever wanted to know about her husband. While secretly accessing Steve's computer, Susan discovered pornographic material that could ruin his career. She found that he was involved in pornographic chat rooms where people flaunted naked body parts and discussed deviant sexual activities, and her husband was more than a spectator in those chat rooms. He was also e-mailing a variety of women while continuing an extramarital affair. Steve was a busy guy with no boundaries.

Susan kept planning and trying to leave him, but she always dithered while trying to gather things together before leaving the house. She never successfully made it out the door. Because her feelings were paramount, she had no resolve. She quivered and swayed like a leaf in the wind, always angry with herself for putting up with her husband. Susan was lost. She and her identity remained a reflector and reactor to Steve.

Susan vowed that she and I would keep in touch as she came and went for therapy, making appointments for several months and then disappearing. However, by entering therapy, she showed that she had sufficient courage to expose her bruised and battered ego but not the strength to dig deeply. She could not extricate and eradicate the powerful ties that kept her embroiled in a destructive relationship. Susan's intellectual and emotional lives had not yet fused.

Susan is still visiting me for therapy, and she is gaining insight and feeling better. In her words, she feels more "like a person." Our connection is important, and I believe therapy will eventually provide a path of knowledge and the backbone she needs to develop a firm sense of self and the strength to make healthy choices.

CHAPTER 8
Manipulative Anger

Karen sounded frantic as she cried hysterically on the phone. Between sobs, she told me that her husband did not understand the relationship between her and a friend. Her husband thought she was having an affair. When Karen calmed down, I asked if her husband was available for marriage counseling. She hesitated and then said, "I have asked him. Sometimes he says yes; sometimes he says no. But I'll ask him again."

The following evening, Karen, a thirty-six-year-old, arrived at my office on time, alone. Her blond hair was pulled back in a thick braid, and very little makeup covered her freckles. She wore cowboy-style clothes—jeans and fringed boots.

Karen began her first session by pleading her case, begging for understanding and, possibly, for forgiveness. Eyes red, Kleenex at the ready, Karen began.

"I have an old friend, Bobby, whom I talk with on the phone. I give him advice. I'm his shoulder to cry on. That is all.

"I just discovered that my husband, Jeff, has been taping my calls and believes that I am having an affair. I love Jeff—I tell him that all the time. I have absolutely no feelings for Bobby."

She wiped her eyes and blew her nose before continuing. "What's more, Jeff has told friends, family, and pretty much anyone he talks with that I'm having an affair. He even took Rachel, our fifteen-year-old daughter, with him to spy on Bobby. I am so mad and so humiliated and so embarrassed.

"Jeff asked me to stop calling Bobby, and I said, 'No. I am not doing anything wrong, and you can't control me.' My first husband was a control freak, among other things, and I won't put up with someone trying to order me around." She looked at me for several seconds and then said, "I'm thinking Jeff wants a divorce, so I'm starting to look for a full-time job. I need to be prepared."

"Do you want a divorce?" I asked.

Puffing herself up, she said, "No, absolutely not. I love my husband and I want the marriage, but I will not be told what to do. I said to Jeff, 'We need marriage counseling.' He said, 'No, not now,' but I know I better have help *now*."

Karen's mantra was "I have the right to talk with a friend. Jeff can't tell me what to do. How dare he intrude on my privacy? He's deliberately turning my phone calls against me."

Those defensive thoughts did not solve Karen's problem, but they did incense her, ramp up her anger, and put her in a combative relationship position.

An hour after Karen left my office, Jeff called and asked for an appointment. We agreed to meet two days later.

Since people are different when they are alone, I meet each marriage partner individually once and indicate that the session is confidential. Occasionally partners keep secrets (such as affairs or previous marriages) or important information from their partners. They fear that to reveal secrets in a joint session will be so shocking or upsetting that their partners will stomp out of treatment.

Jeff

Jeff arrived on time. He was dressed impeccably in a sport coat and tie. He was about five feet seven and small boned; his blond hair was thinning.

He nodded, introduced himself shyly, rearranged his tie, looked around the office nervously, turned, and finally settled into a large leather chair.

To eliminate some of his anxiety, I thought it best to explain a couple of things. "I'm interested not only in your thoughts and feelings about the present problems but also in any other thoughts that come to mind, even if they are historical or seem to be irrelevant to you. I want you to know that I respect and *expect* that both of you will have different perspectives about some of the same problems."

Jeff nodded and was prepared to talk. "This crisis began with a phone bill. It was higher than usual, so I looked at Karen's list of calls—my heart stopped. I was shocked because she had made forty calls to one number— forty calls! Can you imagine? And it was a number I was unfamiliar with.

"Karen is an outgoing person, a chatterbox, and has lots of people calling her and vice versa. She always tells me about her sister's problems or her friends', but I hadn't heard of anyone having a major problem that required forty calls.

"Of course, I dialed the number and got an answering device. I wasn't sure who it was, but the voice clearly belonged to a male. From then on, I became a detective. I looked at old telephone bills, and there was the same number—call after call after call. I felt dizzy and unbalanced."

He stared at me for a moment. "I'm sorry that I did some of the things I did, like confiding in my daughter and talking to everyone in the world. I feel stupid now. I should have kept it to myself. Instead, I proceeded to tape Karen's calls, and what I heard just made me sick. She and this guy talked sexually—explicit sex talk."

I interrupted him. "When you say 'explicit,' what do you mean?"

He twitched. "I have to say that Karen is more sexual than I am; she always initiates sex. What she was saying on the phone freaked me out. I feel embarrassed. My telling you makes it uglier and more disgusting." He had to look away before continuing. "They described which body parts they wanted to touch and what it would feel like."

CAROL L. RHODES PHD

A long pause ensued.

"I'm still crazed. This guy is an old friend whom she says I met once, as if that makes it okay! I also know she slept with him before we were married. Karen claims she doesn't care about him, he's just a friend, but she refuses to stop talking to him; in my opinion, that means she has feelings for him. Why did she keep it a secret if it didn't amount to anything?

"When I try to talk to her about her behavior, she becomes furious with me and tries to turn the situation against me, as if I'm wrong for asking questions. She has always gotten really mad if I criticize her behavior—she always claims that I'm only trying to control her. But this situation? I can't make sense out of it. In a marriage, who talks secretly to another person forty times in one month unless an affair is going on? Karen totally denies it and says I'm nuts. If it's not an affair, what else could you call it?"

An Affair

Thrown into another dimension where he must be on guard and struggling to grasp the unthinkable—that his wife might be unfaithful—Jeff was devastated. He was emotionally fragile, consumed by feelings of betrayal, and unable to calm himself. His mind was a quagmire of quicksand; life as he had known it was gone, the comfort of home a thing of the past. His mind had become unsteady while trying to make what little sense he could out of his nightmare.

The suggestion alone of an affair can rock the stability of life, disrupt the present, and force the past to be questioned. What is real? What is a lie? The foundation of marriage—trust—disappears when the suggestion is made.

Despite a crisis in which the mind grinds to a halt, life goes on. In similar cases, I've seen people struggle to fulfill their ordinary duties once they suspect that their partners were having affairs. Jeff was able to function. He continued to work, to help take care of their kids, and to attend to various chores. His ability to function was a healthy sign.

My main goals during that first session with Jeff was to help him think calmly both in and out of therapy and to establish his primary need in the relationship.

"Right now, you are caught in a nightmare, unable to figure out what is real. Would you say that is correct?" I asked.

Jeff nodded.

"Together, we are going to figure out what's going on. I've been a marriage counselor for twenty-five years, finding solutions and sorting out difficult relationships. You are no longer working on this situation alone. Does that make sense?"

"Karen said you would help us."

"In order to find a way out of these unbearable feelings, let's start with what you want. Do you want the marriage?"

"Yes, I think I do. I still love Karen."

"All right. When you get home today, determine a time when you and your wife can talk quietly without interruptions. Your children must not be present. If she becomes defensive or hysterical, you must stay calm. Your job is to gather information. You need to learn how she feels about the marriage and what she needs from you. You also will be setting a different tone for the relationship. In the conversation, you must establish a different type of connection with her, one in which you are in charge of yourself and can listen to her calmly.

"It will be difficult to remain calm, but keep in mind you are in charge of this conversation. You are not accusatory. As best as you can, ignore her anger. Angry outbursts are a manipulation tactic; they are attempts to distract, dissuade, and interrupt your thoughts. When your wife is talking, you must *not* do several things."

I wrote down and gave him the following list:

- Do not contradict her.
- Do not counter her.
- Do not talk about how you feel.
- Do not condemn her for anything she says.
- Do not interrupt her.
- You may ask for clarification.
- Do not threaten divorce.
- Do not threaten to take the money and the children.

"I realize that these are difficult suggestions to follow. You should keep the list close in case you need to remind yourself of what *not* to do, or you can memorize it. Mainly, just remember that verbalizing your anger will not shed light on the situation.

"When you are by yourself, take charge of your mind. To help you do that keep the following concepts in mind. Try to memorize these as well."

This is the second list I gave him:

- Obsessing about Karen's phone calls must stop immediately.
- Constantly thinking about the phone calls puts your life in the past. Nothing can be done about yesterday.
- When you hear your mind whipping up anguish and anger, tell yourself, "Stop it!"
- Continuously focus on your desire: a happy marriage. Only time will tell whether you can trust Karen.

Karen

Karen's behavior fit the word *affair*, which means an "illicit, secret relationship." No wiggling out of it. The constant phone calls plus phone sex indicated at least an emotional affair. Karen's refusal to stop calling Bobby was peculiar—if she truly wanted her marriage.

Karen had deliberately set herself up for trouble and negative attention. What was her motivation? Was this a telephone "repair affair" meant to get Jeff's attention or the beginning of the end of the marriage? In *Affairs: Emergency Tactics*, by Carol Rhodes, a repair affair is meant to get a partner's attention and change the relationship.

It seems she was going to be true to her right to be independent while she was living in a dependent relationship; she wanted to be loyal to her telephone-sex buddy but not to her husband. Karen said that was how she talked to her female friends. *Unlikely!*

Unwinding Jeff's And Karen's Thought Patterns

Jeff had an ongoing experience of distress justified by external reality. His bitterness was bubbling and boiling as his inner dialogue seethed with anger and resentment toward Karen. Could Jeff redirect his thought processes?

Jeff stated that he loved Karen and wanted the marriage. Karen stated that she loved Jeff and wanted the marriage. Did their thoughts corroborate their words? Were their words real or the fear of loss?

Could Jeff calm his brain through this troubled period?

Karen, Decide What You Want

I told Karen that she first needed to decide what she wanted. If she genuinely wanted the marriage, then she must do the following:

- Acknowledge your telephone calls. Stop using defensive maneuvers in which you claim that you are innocent. Stop blasting your husband with anger or suggesting he is wrong to suggest an affair.
- Being impulsive and angry is your forte. Bring the emotional escalator to a halt by paying attention to your own negatively

charged thoughts, which whip up your anger. Replace them with a mantra of calm and patience. Force patience.

- A powerful technique for instant change is physical action. Walk around the house, walk or run outside, do push-ups, lift weights, any activity will do.
  a. Use the one-minute rule.
  b. Put negative thoughts on paper, then tear them up and throw the paper and the thought away. Negative thoughts are to be discussed with your therapist only, not with friends.

In response, Karen said, "I know Jeff will bring up Bobby, and then what should I do?"

"Acknowledge that Jeff's thoughts and feelings are difficult for him. Do not respond defensively. You are a grown woman in control of your thoughts, words, and behavior. Take control of yourself, and focus on the fact that your husband is in distress."

Jeff said the same thing: "I can't pretend that everything is okay. I can't spend a day with Karen and ignore what she has done."

"Well," I said, "I guess finding a solution is hopeless. Both of you are leaves in the wind without control. When you are at work, do you say every word that comes to mind or stay riveted on one thought?

"Quit talking to yourselves as though you have been programmed by this situation and cannot change. If you want your marriage to change, you must change. There isn't any magic, and you know it. Take control one minute, one hour, and one day at a time."

Train The Brain

The possibility of an affair damages trust, which is the foundation of a committed relationship, and may crack trust permanently. To reestablish trust, Karen had to cut Bobby and their phone calls out of her life, and when her mind wandered into lame defenses (such as her thinking, "I will not be controlled"), she needed to realize that she was rationalizing. She could not have it both ways—that is, she could either stay married and committed or get a divorce and remain free to have phone liaisons with the opposite sex.

First, Karen walked a straight marital path and stopped her denying and rationalizing. Second (and this is crucial), she understood and learned how to feed her need for attention by using positive, healthy, life-affirming ways rather than by seeking the attention of other men. Karen also reinforced her love for Jeff daily. He was the one and only man in her life.

Jeff lifted a corner of his trauma and focused on the ideas that Karen was unusual, that he had always trusted her and known that she would say and do anything, and that those phone calls did not constitute an affair. Jeff did not allow his mind to retort with any ifs, ands, or buts.

It was easy to see that Jeff's and Karen's thoughts were their lives. In crises, we become primitive and repeat dramatic words to ourselves over and over as we try to find a way to escape the horror of the trauma. The emotional escalator is in motion: winding emotions up and down, up and down.

Conscious awareness is always available. Take charge, catch, and stop the emotionally distressing thoughts.

Day Alone

"Try a day alone with each other. Plan a day alone without children, phones, or responsibilities. On the day alone, you are not allowed one negative word. Marital history should not be discussed. If a negative thought comes to either of your minds, it is not allowed out of your mouth.

"Do *not* plan the day if you know you cannot follow through with these ideas: Think of the day alone as a peak performance in your marriage, searching for flow. You will act toward your spouse in exactly those ways that you want from your spouse—without expectations that this should be what your partner is giving to you.

"A day alone with a positive, loving focus is a breather, an opportunity to look and think about one another without interruption. At the end of the day, when you are walking back into your responsible lives again, plan daily words and behaviors to stay on a loving track."

Solution

Working through their issues was difficult and, at times, felt hopeless, but Karen and Jeff stuck with it and are now together, one year after their marriage counseling ended. They reported that Karen has stopped phoning or accepting calls and learned to "shut up." Jeff does not bring up her relationship with Bobby. They do not talk about the past. If a hint of past talk pops up, they walk away from one another. They have even stopped and gotten out of the car to change a mental set.

Heather, on the other hand, is not doing well. She recently discovered a secret that put her long-term marriage in jeopardy.

CHAPTER 9
Anger Solves Problems

People who act on their belief that anger solves problems are blind and deaf and unaware of the enormous cost of anger. Spewing anger relieves their tension and anxiety momentarily, but the fallout after scorching a partner with blame, disgust, or any ugly, uncontrolled emotion results in alienation, hurt, and long-term scarring.

Heather
Oblivious to feelings other than her own, Heather managed her children and husband with high-pitched emotions and anger—it was her way or the highway. She was always right and had the solution to every problem.

Heather and Bob
After twenty-five years of marriage, Bob would not respond to Heather for days on end. Bob had always been the strong, silent type, but for the last few months before the therapy sessions began, whenever Heather

tried to talk with Bob or ask him questions, he simply stared and turned away.

To get his attention, Heather followed him around the house, explaining her distress, talking loudly, yelling, and demanding that he talk to her. Instead, he used his car to escape.

In desperation, Heather asked for marriage counseling...alone. "I need to tell someone the whole story and get some help for Bob."

First Therapy Session

Heather bustled into my office, introduced herself, plopped down on the couch, and indicated she would like to start the session by giving me information. "Is that all right?" she asked.

"Yes," I said.

"I'm here because my husband, Bob, who has always been a quiet person, hasn't spoken to me for weeks. I've been trying hard to get his attention, and I am at a point where I'm out of control. I just can't stop myself. I raise my voice, yell, and curse; then either I stomp out of the room, or he leaves the house."

A solidly built and attractively dressed fifty-year-old, Heather was tearing up while describing her life with Bob. "I'm scared. Bob has gone into a shell, and I'm afraid he is going to lose his job. He's a CPA. He supervises fifty people, and if he doesn't engage, he will lose his job.

"I can't stand the silent treatment. Bob's never initiated a talk, but he would at least respond. We're building a new house, and he won't even answer questions about the house. You know that when you're building a house, there are a million details that have to be decided. He has been totally blank."

"It seems that partners who are building a new house would not have difficulty talking with each other," I said.

After blowing her nose, Heather said, "I know it. The situation doesn't make sense, but I'm sick of it! I've been screaming at him. He just looks at me and walks away. I've always gotten mad and yelled, but his behavior is ridiculous. I'm way over the edge with my anger."

She sat up straight and planted her feet on the carpet before continuing. "I threaten divorce, threaten to tell everyone about his behavior, and threaten to turn our grown children against him." She looked straight at me as though expecting an argument. "My marriage to Bob has always been stable and solid until this distancing act of his.

"To give you an idea of his personality, I have to be the emotional conduit for the family. Someone needed to be, and Bob doesn't show any emotion. When I complain about his behavior, my grown kids come right out and tell me I'm the problem—they say I'm overbearing, bossy, and angry. I constantly tell our children that their father won't take charge and never has and that his failure to do so makes me look like a villain."

Heather's voice accelerated. "In my defense, I had to get his attention somehow, and raising my voice seemed to be the only way!"

Defensive and feeling sorry for herself, Heather said she told her adult children, "I filled the vacuum when your dad refused to take part in disciplining or even talking to you. I used what I knew, Grandma's tell-it-like-it-is style."

"You feel alone and unappreciated," I said. "Your husband is withdrawn; he acts as if you don't exist. And your usual method of solving problems is not working."

"Yes. I continuously rack my brain, always trying to understand what the problem is and what changed. I'm a fourth-grade teacher. You can imagine how busy I am not only with the expectations of parents and the principal but also with after-school activities. I won't even go into that. Nothing has changed for me, but Bob has mentally checked out."

"Heather, it sounds as if you are a person who looks at a problem and then gets busy trying to find a solution. Since your husband has shut down and is turning a deaf ear to your frustration and mounting anger, it's time to calm down, step back, and reassess the situation. Let's consider some other possibilities."

Heather stared at me, ignoring the message that she should think in other ways. She was baffled and focused on what she viewed as an accusation. "What do you mean about my anger? That's how my family is. Everyone knows I get over it, and so do they. Everyone gets angry—it's natural."

Though offered an opportunity to reflect on her situation, Heather demonstrated an aversion to accepting new insight. She doubled down in holding her position. She believed that when she spoke and her husband did not respond as she wanted him to, he was wrong. Because she felt right, she would let herself talk louder to help him understand whatever she was trying to say. She did not understand the idea that yelling at him in anger was not in her best interest.

However, in the next session, Heather reported having had enough insight to initiate affection, understanding that sex was a priority to Bob. "I seldom had time for Bob, especially when he began his romance routine. Sex was the last thing on my mind but the first thing on Bob's. I really was too tired and totally not into sex. I realize I never focused my attention on what he wanted. I just thought...I don't know...I really never thought about Bob.

"But I've changed. Last week, when I tried to kiss and hug him, he walked away. I think Bob is depressed or having some kind of midlife crisis or a nervous breakdown.

"Oh, by the way, Bob moved out," she said calmly and nonchalantly. But within seconds, she seemed to think it over and brought out a high-pitched, hysterical voice and said, "I can't believe he's gone!"

"I notice that your emotions change quickly. Are you ambivalent about his leaving?"

She paused and rubbed her eyes. "Well, I think I'm sick of worrying and wondering what's going on with him."

The Sleuth

Heather then focused on her main question: what *is* wrong with Bob? She had tried to give him what he had seemed to want, but he denied her offer. She became Sherlock Holmes, inspecting his bank statements, his credit card activities, his mail, and (when she could manage it) his phone. She found the reason for Bob's withdrawal. The withdrawal's name was Joanne.

Heather was furious. She could not believe that Bob was involved with a "piece of s—— like Joanne."

Now Heather knew and understood the problem. Now what? She was stuck, depressed, and understandably unable to let go of the fury that fueled her mind and body, causing her to wallow in disgust and anger at her husband's affair. In therapy, it was evident that her confident, in-your-face presentation had crumbled: her clothes looked slept in, and the snappy, bossy style had slipped away. Sniffling off and on, wiping her eyes, blowing her nose, she reported that she could not sleep, eat, and work.

The discovery of her husband's affair brought Heather's normal life to a screeching halt, producing a mental and physical crisis. "I can't think straight," she said. "One minute I could kill him because I'm so angry. The next I'm a blubbering mess."

Fear and Anger

Heather's anger was based on fear. She grew up as one of six siblings, and each birthday was barely a year apart from the next. Her father worked two jobs. Her mother, overwhelmed by six children, used fear tactics to maintain control. Discussions were not a part of their family life; there were no warm and fuzzy hugs, no questions about how anyone was feeling.

Heather said, "In our house, there was a lot of yelling and hitting. Mom always threatened us by saying, 'When your father gets home, you'll really be in trouble.' We did our jobs or else. The *else* was slapping, paddling, or going to bed without dinner. The older siblings were blamed if the younger kids got in trouble. Everyone was always mad at everyone else."

"To survive in your family, you had to develop a thick skin, be able to strike back verbally and physically, be able to bully siblings, and be able to hide your feelings. You learned to strike first and fast, but those behaviors are no longer helpful."

Heather began to sob loudly, hiccupping, wanting to talk but unable to do so. She pulled herself together after several minutes and said, "I feel so sorry for my little-girl self." She sniffled some more and then, surprisingly, she said, "I guess it's time. Something has to change."

The Project

Exhausted by her emotional struggle, Heather seemed to switch tactics. She turned her attention away from fixing Bob and focused on how to bring him back.

"Anger is not going to bring him back," I said. "If you have a feeling, you react without thinking. Correct?"

Heather nodded.

"How do you intend to bring him back? If you do not respond as you did in the past, how will you respond? Exactly what will you say?"

"I'll be nice to him."

To be nice to her husband, Heather began a daily conscious and deliberate attempt to gain control of her thoughts and behavior. The first thing she decided to tackle was her automatic anger trigger.

Thoughts

Thoughts create feelings; feelings generate behavior. If you change your thoughts, you will change your behavior. In the past, Heather told her husband what to do, and if he did not take action, she would think, "That makes me mad. He wants me to be upset—how dare he!" Such thoughts were rooted and buried in her subconscious and were no longer accessible to her after years of marriage, so they became angry feelings. She responded to her feelings with wild explosions, blurting out intense, angry words, along with ugly expressions that she was attempting to control.

Struggling With Change

For Heather, retraining her brain was a daunting task but doable if she remained dedicated. Since Heather learned at her mother's knee that anger was power and could be used indiscriminately, her anger was like breathing, substituting reason for anger would be difficult. Using the intellect to make changes requires relentless, conscious focus on positive desires.

Because changes in the brain cannot be seen, determination to change thoughts often falters. Although a muscle is no more apparent to the naked eye than the brain, to focus on physical development requires action—just like lifting weights. We've all seen proof of that concept, the proof being the muscle-bound weight lifters. Another example of the unseen but deliberate brain change is a child who continuously repeats multiplication tables and soon has them memorized for life. Changing the neural connections in the brain for any reason requires the same repetition.

For example, London taxi drivers must know the name of every street in the city before they are licensed. A study by University College London was taken before potential drivers began to study streets and then again after their licensing, and the study demonstrated that parts of the brain linked to memory grew larger, which is proof that the brain actually grows with focus and determination.

Brains have the potential to build new neurons, and that means anger habits engraved in the brain can be eliminated or rerouted and replaced by thoughtful, calm ideas. It is important to prime your mind with this information: emotions and intellect are tied together. The time, energy, and powerful determination required to alter habitual anger responses require constant, conscious energy. Keep these three concepts in mind:

- Anger should be viewed as a virus.
- Anger is your enemy, not your friend.
- Your mind is powerful. Use conscious, peaceful thoughts as medication to sooth and calm your brain.

If you decided to exercise, you would make sure you had the proper clothing, equipment, schedule, and time determinations. The same is true with brain changes.

Action
Follow the following list to help you break through your angry habits:

- Think ahead and practice when you are alone or socializing.
- Recognize, catch, and eliminate angry thoughts.
- When anger rises in the middle of a sentence, turn away. If you doubt your ability to look away—tell yourself that you can.
- Take three deep breaths.
- Replace your angry thoughts will optimistic ones, such as "I love Bob. He loves me."

- At every opportunity, write down your thoughts, in the morning, at noon, or at night. You need to clarify your thought processes. Get rid of fuzzy thinking:
  a. Bring the loving plan into consciousness at every opportunity.
  b. Look squarely at anger's crushing damage. If you don't care how others feel, keep it up.

When the urge to purge unpleasant thoughts enters your brain, relax, catch, and replace the thought with something positive about the person or situation.

It is critical when you begin a mind-altering plan that you understand that adhering to the plan is difficult because the mind initially resists change. We are lazy. Like babies, we do not want to put effort into change. Our minds often shout at us and say, "Why should I have to do this? It isn't fair!"

Stop it! Keep in mind that success far outweighs giving in and giving up.

This is where determination and mental strength shine. Think about your goal when you get up, before you go to sleep, and when you are eating breakfast, lunch, and dinner. Keep the process churning: put sticky notes on your windshield and on your bathroom mirror. Any new behavior begins with enthusiasm and focus. For example, imagine that you are dieting. All of a sudden, your goal slips your mind, and you find yourself munching on a delicious dessert—whoops! Oh well.

No *whoops* are allowed. You have the stamina and mental resolve to carry out your goal.

I wanted Heather to deeply consider the following important issues and for us to talk about them:

1. Keep your plan in mind.
   - Listen to others.
   - Bob has a right to his thoughts and feelings.

- Maintain your calm, whether he speaks or not.
- Silence is golden. You do not have to fill silent lapses.
- Before you speak, use your intellect to examine your thoughts and put negative feelings aside.

2. Are these the outcomes you want in your life?
   - Others do what you want when you get angry.
   - Control of others is powerful and feels good. Are you the gestapo? Must you order people around?
   - You think you know best. Why?
   - Anger arouses fear. Fear as a communication method does not work. It's a dictatorship.

3. Take responsibility.
   - "I have a right to be angry; my mother was angry with me."
   - Are you a child?
   - Are you always right and others wrong?
   - Acknowledge that you have been an anger bully.

4. Blaming others.
   - Bob is responsible for your anger. If he did not act or react in certain ways, did not speak softly or speak loudly, did not have ideas of his own, you would not respond with anger.
   - Others deliberately goad you into a rage.
   - You know best—they know nothing.

5. Allow yourself to have feelings other than anger.
   - You fear emotional closeness. Anger keeps others away.
   - Love does not mean others must do as you say.

Wrapping Up

Heather reported that her working on becoming an insightful person, her living inside out, her taking time to think through issues, and her examining her own behavior instead of immediately reacting were challenging tasks. She struggled and was often mad that she was the one who had to make changes.

Nevertheless, Heather dismissed and reworked the angry thoughts that kept popping up. Her martyr-like past told her that she had done everything; Bob was only an observer who sat back and was not involved in household tasks or disciplining the children. Letting go of these old habitual thoughts was difficult. Currently, however, Heather has been growing and changing. She has grasped the fact that her behavior plays a major role in their marital problems, and she has made a huge leap into thinking maturely and taking responsibility for her life.

Because Heather wants the marriage and thinks Bob is not dedicated to his mistress, she has been modifying her behavior for months, learning to control her anger. Heather "allows" Bob to be silent, without recriminations.

At this time, their relationship has no intimacy, sex, or shared feelings, but there is peace and thus potential. If her husband hears a hint of her boss-tone, he leaves. Although Bob is living with his brother, the comfort of home calls to him, and he is often home with Heather, speaking with her and carrying on conversations.

CHAPTER 10

Anger as a Communication Style

Communication is generally a huge problem in marriages. Couples often avoid talking about feelings, argue instead of talking rationally to resolve issues, speak with harsh attitudes, do not speak because they fear angry free-for-alls, and use silence to inflict punishment.

Two consequences that stem from the lack of free and open communication are frustration and anger. In the case of Denise and Dan, either their anger rumbled beneath the surface, or open hostility erupted without warning.

The First Session

After gathering preliminary information from Denise and Dan at our first meeting, I asked, "What brings you in?"

Denise looked at Dan, waited a few seconds, and then said, "We're unhappy. We just can't talk. Once upon a time, Dan and I were able to communicate; in fact, we talked like magpies, but somehow we disconnected early on. I don't know what happened."

Silence ensued.

To make them feel comfortable, I said, "I'm interested in present problems and historical family-relationship issues," but before I could continue, Dan interrupted me.

"Excuse me," he said, leaning forward, "but before we start with our respective histories, I think you should know what prompted my call to you. On Sunday, I confronted Denise. She's having Internet sex chats with a male coworker. I don't know what to call it. I don't know if that's all it is or if it's a full-blown affair." He fell back on the couch.

Silence, again.

Denise turned to stare at Dan. "What are you talking about?" she said, nearly barking. "I told you I have no interest in Jim."

"Come on, Denise. I have copies of everything you and Jim have discussed. I'm sick every day that it goes on. And the guy is a coworker—are you nuts? What do you want? Do you want a divorce?" His face had turned red, and his hands were shaking.

"All right, I admit I was wrong. I'm sorry." Her tone was agitated rather than imploring. Ignoring her husband, keeping her eyes on me, she said, "I told Dan last night I made a mistake. I won't do it again, but he doesn't listen. He's making a huge deal out of it. I do not want to fight with him again. We had a monstrous fight last night—no, nothing physical."

"You don't call throwing things physical?" Dan asked.

"Well, I mean we didn't physically hit one another. Dan never listens to me. I have to shriek to get his attention; then he starts to rage and we fight. Dan is in his own world, and I suppose that's why this happened. I really don't know what possessed me; talk on the net is so stupid.

"I tried to defend myself last night. I'm lonely, and Dan knows it. He is up and gone at the crack of dawn. It's late when he gets home. He ignores me because he's exhausted, and then he falls asleep—and that's it. Or he's traveling.

"I feel like I don't have a marriage. No one is ever home. I mean, I feel as though I have no connection mentally or physically with anyone. Right now, what upsets me more than anything else is that Dan has known about this Internet situation for several weeks but has not said anything about it. If he actually cared about me, he would have confronted me instead of sneaking around and copying my e-mails."

Affair Fallout

Whether emotional or sexual, whether meant to end or repair a partnership, an affair calls a halt to normal activities. Denise cleverly (and I assume unconsciously) found a way to get her husband's attention. She arranged for him to accidentally find incriminating e-mails between her and her coworker.

From the moment of discovery, a switch had been turned on in Dan's mind. During the days and nights, real and imagined facts of the affair steamrolled in, splattering and fragmenting peace between the couple.

As therapy progressed, it became clear that Denise used her own boredom and disinclination to take action as an excuse for her dissatisfaction with her life. She blamed Dan for her unhappiness and made it his responsibility to improve her life. This maneuver further solidified her unhappiness; her focus was on getting Dan to do for her what she needed to do for herself.

Dan rejected his role as the one meant to make Denise happy. She then got angry and attacked his character and behavior, and Dan shut down and made himself scarce emotionally and physically. As his efforts to appease Denise failed, such as his buying jewelry for her or suggesting lavish vacations, she used her mother's modus operandi and did her best to remove whatever self-esteem Dan had left. In short, while she deplored her "snarky, cranky mother," she imitated the woman's behavior.

Dan's History

As a child, Dan learned that males in his family were not allowed to display their emotions. If he was weepy, he was told things like "knock it off or I'll give you something to cry about" or "big boys don't cry." The message was constant: weakness could not be tolerated.

Dan was seven when his mother died from a drug overdose. He never really knew his father. Dan's aunt (his mother's sister) and her husband (a psychiatrist) adopted him and provided for his physical needs, but his cousins and uncle ignored him. He was an outsider.

Predictably, by the time Dan was twelve, he was diagnosed as depressed and spent hours going from one psychologist or psychiatrist to another. Withdrawn, he seldom spoke and was not interested in anyone or anything. Although he had an above-average IQ, he was a borderline student.

As an adult, Dan found his niche as a salesman, where he was superficially close to others. He met Denise and quickly fell in love with her, and their marriage was just around the corner. The honeymoon was over in a matter of months because Denise's needs had become paramount. His work required travel, and Denise began a campaign to have him home more because she "needed him." She began nagging him to spend more time with her, come home earlier, and quit traveling, always insisting that he make her feel loved.

Dan—puzzled, frustrated, confused, and caught in the double bind of having to travel for his work but be at home to satisfy his wife—felt helpless. The depression returned, and Dan shut down emotionally as Denise intensified her attacks. She complained about how miserable life was with him, and his misery penetrated deep into his core.

Denise's History

Denise's mother was a narcissist; her father, an alcoholic. Narcissists view the world only from their perspective; other people are extensions of themselves with no true individual existence. Narcissistic personalities need to be powerful, to dominate, to humiliate if necessary, and to get their way regardless of the feelings or interests of other people.

Narcissistic traits alongside alcoholism produce needy, angry, and confused children who are damaged emotionally and developmentally. Denise's massive problems with her mother and father left her severely deprived of love and attention and devoid of the relationship skills that provide satisfaction and maturation.

Facing the Facts

In close relationships, it is difficult to understand the dynamics that fuel the problems. Denise and Dan had come face to face with each other's character issues. Denise had chosen a distant person, and since they married, she had been in the business of turning Dan into a loving, thoughtful homebody to suit her own needs. Of course, that was not working.

Denise said, "I don't want to change Dan." However, that was exactly what she was trying to do with her behavior. "It's just that this is not the person I started out with. Where did he go?" She seemed to think that if she kept chipping away at him, the real Dan—that is, the desired Dan—would emerge.

Denise wanted Dan to be a mind reader. "He should know I need attention. If he cared, he would listen and understand my feelings," she said. From Denise's perspective, Dan's failure to listen was evidence of two possibilities: either her feelings were not important to him, or he deliberately withheld from her what she craved—just like her parents had done.

Dan was clueless about what drove Denise. His family history had subconsciously taught him that his job in any partnership was to work and to show he cared by buying jewelry and making money. In his marriage with Denise, he was swimming in a sea of emotional chaos, which was making him physically ill. The stress had taken over and was affecting him in various ways: he was suffering from stomachaches, diarrhea, back pain, headaches, depression, and anxiety. His emotions had sickened his body.

Possible Solution

Was there hope for this couple? If so, it would begin with an admission of the Internet affair. Denise had to stop her angry outbursts that were aimed at getting Dan's attention or at diverting attention from her behavior. If Dan was limited to salving his wounded ego and Denise was unwilling to own up to her activities, the game would be over—that is, the relationship would end. If she actually regretted the affair and genuinely loved Dan and if she wanted to save and enhance their relationship, then she would have to tell the truth and nothing but the truth and hope that it was not too late.

Reviving the Marriage

Marriage counseling often requires a review of the past to understand the present and to create a preferred future. Many troubles in the present can be traced to the forces in a person's earlier life, and those forces often linger and survive to the present and negatively affect new relationships. If Denise and Dan did not learn why they were continually angry, disappointed with their situation in life, depressed, and anxious, they would be doomed to repeat their dysfunctional behaviors and defend them with rationalizations.

Finding a new mate is likely to provide a new situation in which to act out old patterns. Such behavior can be termed a repetition compulsion. For example, people often end relationships because their mates do not give them enough attention, and then they find new mates who end up doing the same thing.

If that was true of Denise, she would substitute another person and eventually repeat her temper tantrums and angry words. She would offend the new partner by blaming him. Repeating the process would only show just how hurt she had been as a child, when she could only get her distant, apathetic mother's attention by having an emotional meltdown.

For Dan, the seeds of depression were planted at age seven. That year, Dan's father abandoned the family, his drug-addicted mother died, and he was adopted by his aunt's unpleasant family, who promptly ignored him. His need for love and attention unfulfilled ever since childhood, Dan once again slid into his known safe place—depression—when he was bombarded by Denise's angry disapproval and blatant betrayal.

In Dr. Aaron T. Beck's book *Depression: Causes and Treatment*, he provides insight into the underlying reasons for Dan's type of depression: "A depressed self-image can be characterized by the four D's: Defeated, Defective, Deserted, and Deprived."

These feelings develop in part as a result of distorted negative thinking and illogical pessimistic attitudes; they are meant to help cure life disturbances through brain chemistry and neurotransmitters, just like the antibodies that rush to the scene of a cut to begin the healing process.

To sooth Dan and begin problem solving, his system slipped into a depressed state in which his thoughts slowed down and stumbled over one another. What made sense one moment made no sense the next; his perceptions became twisted, one sided, or just plain wrong. This state sounds convoluted and ironic (a person has to feel worse to feel better), but whether this experience is new and traumatic or the revival of old issues, it is worked through by rehashing and reworking a painful problem-solving process.

Depression is also physiological. Dan needed to check with a doctor to make sure that all was well physically and to receive medication if necessary. He needed to exercise, eat healthy food, and remind himself as often as possible that his painful feelings would dissipate with time. He needed to establish positive habits of mind and body as part of his healing process.

Combating Depression and Anger

When Dan and Denise were able understand that their thoughts created anger, depression, and other feelings that were being triggered by their present situation but were connected to the past, they would have choices.

They could choose to continue on the same path of unproductive thinking or take control. If Dan and Denise replaced their distorted thoughts with other more realistic and functional thought processes, their irritability would lessen, and they would gain the ability to focus and listen to one another. Truly listening would allow them to process whatever was being said and attribute the information to the speaker, rather than listening and reacting to distorted conversations in their individual minds.

The idea that their relationship's turmoil was in their control sounded crazy. For example, Denise said, "I get angry for good reasons. I am deliberately provoked sometimes."

Dan said, "Depressed feelings take over. I try to combat them, but I don't have the energy. Besides, I don't know what to do."

"The fact is that as human beings, you *are* subject to emotional turmoil, but your interpretation of events creates your feelings," I said.

When Denise pleaded with Dan for time and attention and he ignored her, her defense was anger. Although anger had not solved problems in her past, she was convinced that showing Dan her feelings for the hundredth time would somehow produce a different outcome. Dan, amid the overwhelming distress, always opted out; he would become moody and refuse to speak. Then he would turn on himself.

"The critical issues are the desire to communicate and the ability to alter interactions," I said. "You both can accept personal responsibility for the tenor of the relationship or repeat ad infinitum the same thoughts and behaviors that solve nothing. The latter option would be crazy. In other words, start with yourselves. People become powerful when they take charge of themselves. You both know you cannot change each other. However, you can keep your minds under control, blank out old thoughts, and calmly acknowledge the other person's ideas and feelings, though you might not agree—though you might even be right!"

If Denise and Dan's ultimate goal was to establish a successful relationship, they had to understand the specific thought distortions that were generating problems. To gain insight and control over those harmful thoughts, they needed to catch the beginning feelings of anger or depression. I told them to see if those thoughts and feelings matched the following distortions:

1. Magnification: If a negative event is exaggerated, the intensity and duration of the emotional reaction are blown out of proportion. A partner bombards his or her own mind with negative thoughts that exacerbate negative feelings. An example of this kind of thought would be "why does he do that? That really makes me mad—I won't put up with that!"

2. Labeling: When people resort to name calling, whether in their minds or out loud, they intensify negative feelings toward the recipients. A smart mother or father will not say, "You are bad." Instead, that parent will say something like "I love you, but I don't approve of that behavior."

3. Mind reading: This is when people invent reasons in their minds for their partners' behaviors or imagine that the partners already know what they are thinking. If partners do not provide actual

input to each other, they have no way of knowing what the other might be thinking or what is motivating them.

4. Should or Shouldn't: This is when a partner knows what is best for everyone. However, these types of partners only frustrate themselves when others do not dance to their preferred tunes. People have free will and will do what they assume is in their best interest, not someone else's. The partners that think they know best need to be honest and humble. They need to stick with what they know about themselves.

Resistance

Denise and Dan desired change but were clinging to interpersonal patterns that kept them mired in mutual misery. They were not unique in their habit. Marriage-counseling studies have indicated that marriage counseling may produce more resistance in therapy (blocking progress by various means) than individual therapy since blame is handed over to the partner. Each spouse in a counseled couple is used to assigning responsibility to the other spouse for the relevant problems and attempts to convince the other spouse and therapist that his or her own view is correct.

Resistance during therapy is routine, but another method, sabotage, begins on the way home—sometimes in the parking lot. Sabotage is about who said what and why, and it involves a partner becoming furious for having been exposed. The comments of these partners may resemble the following:

- "What do you mean I drink too much?"
- "I've never flirted!"
- "You shouldn't have told her I'm going to quit my job."
- "I'm done. See, marriage counseling doesn't help."

These and other comments dilute and dull any positive effects of therapy sessions, which are meant to stimulate clear thinking and to promote insight. Although people want and need help to keep their partnerships from going under, they are also afraid of change and ego damage; consequently, they often work against themselves.

For example, Denise felt helpless in their marriage; she combated that feeling with her powerful, angry feelings toward Dan. She repeatedly told herself that she was being deprived, disrespected, and ignored, resulting in anger outbursts that not only released her pent-up emotions but also satisfied her need for revenge. The worse Dan was made to feel, the more she experienced her own authenticity. Dan was a captive scapegoat. When he returned her anger, she would rage or fall into a pathetic heap, and her reactions were always his fault.

Anger was tolerated in Denise's original family because that emotion was one of the family's normal methods of communication, but using anger as a tool in her relationship with Dan was a one-way, simplistic, and thoughtless approach. Mind-sets, especially those formed in childhood, are usually *mindless*. Children do not have the insight or experience to think through words and behavior acted out by their families.

In short, since Denise had assigned the troublemaker role to Dan, she felt entitled—even driven—to put him down. Moreover, his withdrawal constituted an additional offense for which he must be punished. Whenever Dan withdrew, Denise redoubled her assaults.

"Denise, when has an outburst of anger helped Dan understand your difficulty with his emotional absence?" I asked.

Silence.

"Finally, he only listens when I'm mad," she said.

"Has your anger improved the relationship?"

"Maybe not, but at least I'm being honest with him. I let him know I'm not going to put up with his shit."

"Are you here, in marriage counseling, to improve your relationship?"

"Yes, but he needs to know—"

"I agree that he needs to know how you feel. I can help you present your thoughts and feelings in a productive way. Are you open to that?"

"Yes."

With Denise somewhat calmed, I wanted to specify some modalities that could improve her communication, but Dan butted in. "Her family are all yellers. It is constant chaos in that household. They are unhappy about everything," he said.

Dan did not realize that he was talking about his relationship. Both Dan and Denise refused to listen to each other and denied their responsibility. They had become masters of resistance.

"Dan, instead of assigning blame to Denise's family, suppose you had said, 'I can see how my wife has learned to deal with her feelings. I'm ready to admit I do the same thing. What are the alternatives that might get us out of this mess?'" I said.

The idea was to suggest alternate thinking and talking possibilities for both Denise and Dan.

Managing Emotions

Behavior-altering goals require mindfulness: you need to know what you want and set up a specific plan to reach those goals. Then you must focus faithfully, minute by minute, hour by hour, day by day, on actions and feelings that will achieve what you have set out to do.

Does that sound difficult? It is. Dieting is a good example. Dieters may start the day with a food plan, but desire and habit are so powerful that by six o'clock, even the intention of controlling portions may have disappeared.

The first path to controlling the mind is a powerful desire to change established mental habits. Lazy, unconscious thinking patterns (angry words, turning to depression) interfere with goals. The message to the self must be concrete and conscious. Then that message must be followed to the letter with the understanding that just as continual exercise will strengthen the body, continuous and conscious focus on desired change will alter mind patterns.

If Denise wanted to get what she craved—Dan's attention—she needed to change her past practices. She needed to make constant assurances to Dan that she loved him and had no interest in her coworker. Angry attacks on Dan's character should be rethought, not reproduced. Rather, it would be wise for Denise to appreciate his work ethic and love the jewelry he thoughtfully bought for her.

If Dan desired peace, loyalty, and love, his first step was to focus his attention on Denise and their relationship. For a salesperson to be successful, he or she must thoroughly know the relevant product and pay attention to the buyer for as long as it takes to make a sale. Dan indicated to Denise that he recognized the frustration she had been experiencing with his workaholic behavior. A lukewarm, half-hearted salesperson or partner was always in danger of losing the sale or losing the other partner.

"Denise, please answer these two questions: Has Dan deliberately set out to hurt your feelings with his workaholic behavior? Do your expressions of anger produce positive outcomes for your relationship?"

Denise guessed that Dan did not mean to hurt her feelings and suspected her anger got his attention but did not solve their problems. "I don't know how to stop being angry. Anger is natural for me—it's part of me. It isn't as if I can tell myself to cut it out and then not feel it again. What am I supposed to do?"

"Excellent question!" I said. "Anger is natural, as is eating, walking, talking, and getting up in the morning. Daily life comprises one decision after another, including the discharge of anger. Although anger is natural, uncontrolled anger is not your friend.

"Taking charge of angry feelings requires time, effort, and commitment; success depends upon daily practice. I see that you are fit. You are an exercise person, right?"

Denise nodded.

"The principle behind building a muscle or developing and maintaining cardiovascular fitness requires daily dedication to an exercise plan. The same is true when a person decides to alter a thought pattern: dedication to the plan is crucial."

"Well," said Denise, shaking her head, "anger just washes over me. I never actually think anything like, 'Hey, at four o'clock, I'm going to get mad.'"

"You're right. Anger is part of your emotional toolbox. When you said, 'Anger just washes over me,' you implied that you are helpless in the face of feelings. On the contrary, you are in charge.

"Everyone has the potential to be angry, and although you feel that those feelings simply take over, the fact is you have created a mind-set, an anger trigger. You feel justified, consumed by the need to let it out. It feels good to rant and rave; your tension melts as you let Dan know exactly how you feel. However, to develop control over these explosive periods will require that you devote tremendous conscious energy to your willpower."

Rooting out negative emotions is difficult since the mind's tendency is to fall back onto comfortable thoughts, even when those thoughts are old, negative, and based in fear. Once fear has gained a foothold, the mind is snared: it will grab that fear and focus on it like a baby, while whining and crying for relief at the same time. A mind in this situation may think, "If *you* just change and do what I want, we will both be happy."

Motivated by the need to solve problems, the mind entertains negative thoughts more often than positive thoughts, but that does not mean those ideas are cemented into place. The mind is fluid and ready to do the person's bidding. It is not trapped with the same thoughts circling around, entering and departing without relief, unless you are a wet noodle and allow the same-old destructive thoughts entry. You are in charge of your mind.

Denise developed a relationship story in which Dan was the monster who deliberately thwarted her needs; then she replayed it over and over, using the "you are responsible for my feelings" approach. She would say or think, "I am miserable because you make me miserable."

Changing her life and taking charge of herself required planting and nurturing positive ideas. Positive thoughts quiver and disappear unless they are planted solidly and fed continuously. The power needed to promote thoughts and feelings that are positive and loving requires focus, energy, and a developed desire for a loving relationship.

"Denise, you say you want to be happy, at peace, and in charge of yourself. Here's how: when negative thoughts about Dan enter your mind, immediately replace them with positive, loving thoughts. Do not entertain—not even for a minute—the old agitated thoughts.

"You have allowed angry thoughts to continually filter into your consciousness; that drumbeat has been preventing you from accepting responsibility for your behavior, keeping you stuck, not allowing you to move forward. You can continue or replace those thoughts with loving, positive thoughts. You have the mind power to take charge of your mind!"

Denise said, "I get it...I get it."

"Are you annoyed?"

"I don't want to be, but I am. I'm mad because I thought getting rid of anger would be simple—it's not. It's hard to control myself; still, I feel dedicated to Dan, and I'm in it for the long haul."

"Good. Dan, I have two important questions: Can you let yourself forgive Denise for her e-mail conversations? Are you willing to take charge of your depressed feelings?"

Dan said Denise's e-mail conversations continuously flowed through his mind. "I do everything to forget them, but I don't know if I can forgive her; that means I can't forgive or forget.

"Depressed feelings? Yes, I want to be free of them; I don't want to take medication or be so down I can't think straight. This situation has thrown me yet again into depression. Depression is like my life management, and I'm sick of it. I understand that therapy has to be a priority for me. The other priority is for me to trust Denise."

"To deliberately forgive and forget your marriage must be critically important to you, important enough to make it a priority—that means time and attention.

"Denise, it is imperative that you indicate definitely to Dan that you are no longer in contact with your coworker and that you put your coworker on your computer's spam list. Since you have nothing to hide, Dan will have access to your computer, just as you will have access to his. Is that something the two of you are willing to do?"

Denise said, "I've already done it."

Dan said, "I'm not sure. I want to put her treason behind, but I don't think I can trust that she won't sneak around behind my back and carry on."

"How can Denise show you that the Internet exchanges are over?" I asked.

Dan shook his head. "I don't know, especially since they work together."

"It may be that you cannot recover from this issue; perhaps the damage is too profound to overcome. Shock shuts the mind down and then throws it into turmoil. Thoughts and feelings that Denise, a person you trusted, chose to deliberately engage in deceit,. that she lied and disappointed you may be unbearable as well.

"The loss of love, comfort, and security goes to the core of a person's being—a little boy without parents to love him is a lost little boy. You, however, through inner fortitude and strength of character, have survived your childhood and marched into adulthood able to love and work."

Tears ran down Dan's face, and he reached for a Kleenex. "I feel lost. I can't think straight. I just can't step away or step out of it. I'm drowning in pain."

Denise reached over and hugged Dan. She said sincerely, "I'm so sorry." They held one another.

Change

"This vulnerable exchange can be the beginning of a new life story, a critical moment, a window in time where healthy relationship choices can be made and reality accepted. Your defenses are down; your egos have vanished; love is available.

"An obstacle to acceptance is awareness. Your partner did not fall out of the sky into your lap. Accept the fact that this partner was your choice. Deliberately bring into consciousness the love that you felt, the love that is often buried beneath unsolved problems.

"Instead of struggling with what you don't like and focusing on negative perceptions, stop struggling! Calm down and think something similar to 'I am not happy with myself or the relationship when thoughts are filled with negativity.' You are in therapy to clarify issues about what has happened and why, as well as how you feel. Now is the time to turn the page, to move on, and to be aware of positive feelings. Consciously talk to yourselves about what you want. Accept the past. You cannot change it—it is over. You can change this moment in time."

I gave the following goals to Denise and Dan to keep the therapy moving forward:

- If you need to vent anger, promise yourselves that instead you will walk around the block, do push-ups, read a book, or go to the store. Keep your mouths shut!
- Listen without interrupting.
- Talk one at a time. Think through your responses. Do not blurt out every thought that comes to mind. Since each human has about sixty thousand thoughts a day, chose your words carefully.
- Do not sneer, roll your eyes, or do anything else that might tell a negative story.

Happy Ending

Their marriage survived and is currently thriving. Denise has accepted Dan's quiet personality and job constraints, and she has given up her disturbing, angry rants; she definitely has achieved a substantial measure of growth and development. She also lets Dan know daily that she loves him.

Dan has forgiven Denise's e-mail affair, although he confessed it still comes to mind. However, he does not let himself dwell on it. He has learned to be attentive and to talk with her. Both make it a point to listen to the other and accept differences—without objecting or over-riding each other's points of view.

CHAPTER 11
Walking-in-the-Door Anger

The following story is about another emotionally disturbed marriage that almost went up in flames after Internet deceit was discovered. Anger, an ongoing issue, is often the response to a disturbing discovery.

Laura and Zachary

Zachary phoned for a marriage-counseling appointment, stating that his marriage needed "tweaking." He said that he and his wife had been married eight years and that "although we get along well and enjoy each other's company, we do have a variety of problems that need fixing." And then he asked an interesting question: "Do you have any trouble working with men?"

"Why do you ask?"

He hemmed and hawed and finally said, "Well, I was afraid you might side with my wife since you are female."

Zachary was clever to put me on guard. In effect, he was saying, "Be nice to me." At the same time, gender prejudice was a reasonable fear. I told him I viewed myself as gender invisible. However, in therapy (where it is important to be honest), he was free to let me know if it appeared that I was favoring his wife. He had a good point—there are psychologists who are more comfortable with one gender or the other.

Because Zachary and his wife, Laura, worked long hours, our appointment was in the evening, when both should have been tired. Instead, they were revved up and eager to tell their story, stumbling over one another to talk. Both were thirty-three and presented themselves in alert, anxious manners. Both had no interest in separating. In fact, they had recently built a house together and loved it.

Laura was nice looking, conservatively dressed, and soft spoken. Zachary's red hair was graying; he had the bearing of a sales professional—that is, he was somewhat flamboyant and had lots to say.

After the introductions and before I could ask anything specific, Laura, visibly upset, said, "The reason we're here is...I saw something on the computer that shocked me. I seldom use our home computer, mainly because I work on a computer all day, so even looking at our home computer translates to work.

"I digress. Last Thursday, Zach was working late, and it so happened that I had to connect with my office via our home computer. There had been a glitch at work, which I won't go into. Anyway, when I brought up the screen, I came face to face with a good-looking blonde. Naturally, I checked her out a little more, and the blonde turned out to be part of a dating network. I was shocked. Even though no one was around, I could feel my face flushing, my heart pounding. I don't know what else was happening because I couldn't think. My brain stopped. What in the world had Zach been doing on a website for dating?

"Of course, I assumed that he was probably unhappy with me and was looking for a way out of the marriage or, at least, a diversion. At that moment, divorce was the answer for me."

Staring at her husband, Laura said, "I was devastated. The minute Zach walked in the door, I jumped on him. I was upset and wanted answers. He said he had no idea where the picture had come from or where the site had come from; he was as shocked as I was."

By then, Laura was crying. "Well, how could he be innocent?" she said. "He dashed to the computer, erased the site, shut down the Internet connection, and closed the computer. And then we started to argue in earnest. Even now, he will deny any involvement or guilt. Why did he shut down the computer? That doesn't make sense to me. Why didn't he start checking it out if he's as innocent as he pretends? I think he's lying."

Zachary sputtered and tried to get a word in while Laura talked. When his chance came, he quickly changed the subject. "I'm glad we're here. We've got a lot more problems than the Internet, as far as I'm concerned. First of all, Laura won't kiss me—can you believe that? Since we married, she won't kiss. I need hugging, kissing, and affection." He was too timid to say sex at that point. "She has an anger problem," he said, nodding at Laura. "When she comes home from work, she will dig into me about random things, sometimes things as simple as setting the table wrong." In a slightly different tender tone, he said, "Naturally, she has to vent to me. Who else? Laura's family is not supportive. Her father is a liar." He turned to Laura. "Laura will tell you that's true."

Laura nodded agreement.

"Her sister, well, that's another story."

I found it interesting and pertinent that Laura was possibly faced with a lying husband after living life with a lying father.

Zachary said, "Not that my family is wonderful. My father is an alcoholic. I left home at sixteen and had to figure out how to survive, and I only see my family once or twice a year. We have to have dinner with her dad every Saturday, and I just hate the way he treats Laura."

Zachary continued to speak, and while talking, he continually looked at Laura, patted her arm, and nodded at her—gestures that implied he needed agreement. "Laura lived at home until she was twenty-five. I don't know how she survived mentally with that father. He tells ridiculous stories and makes outrageous statements that you can't refute because he is a lying nutcase." Zachary again patted Laura and nodded, and again she did not disagree when he talked about her father. "He just drives me to distraction," said Zachary.

It seemed that Zachary was getting his ducks in order and his defenses ready before heading into the Internet issue. Zachary was hoping that the Internet would become a nonissue since there was no evidence that he had been anything but reliable and truthful.

Therapy

With each succeeding therapy session, Laura became calmer about Zach and the online-dating issue. Since Laura was a computer person, she knew how to retrieve lost computer material, and thus far her frantic search for evidence had been unproductive. Zach's position continued to be one of innocence, pointing out that sites simply pop up.

Therapy Results

Laura's sudden realization that her peaceful life had disappeared with a glance at her computer was like being hit by a truck. Laura's discovery shocked her out of her habitual patterns of thought, causing her to feel unloved and unsure of herself, intensifying her anger issues.

Although she reported having tearful and fearful days, she was focusing on improving the marriage by controlling her cranky, angry feelings and making a concentrated effort to be affectionate.

Zachary was shaken when Laura pointed out his "failings." He always relaxed in a chair until Laura arrived from work, he expected her to be the cleaning lady, shopping person, and cook, even though her commute to work was an hour longer than his. Though feeling put out and angry, Laura played her part in that scenario by doing the cooking and cleaning.

In therapy, Laura and Zachary figured out how to safely talk about feelings, set up a household schedule with evenly distributed chores, and essentially eliminated their ongoing, nagging problems that had been causing daily bouts of anger.

The online-dating issue was never entirely clarified, but Laura decided she had gone as far as she could go with her investigations and resolved to put the issue aside.

CHAPTER 12
Trigger Anger

Brian called my office and asked for an emergency appointment. When he arrived, he was agitated and short of breath. "I desperately need help!" he said. "Yesterday, I turned on the computer to check out a friend's website, and I couldn't believe my eyes. I felt nauseated when I saw it! It was a sex scene from what must be a porn site for dating. My wife was naked in a sexual pose. I was in shock; I began to sweat. I felt as if I was going into cardiac arrest.

"Then I rushed around looking for my wife and confronted her with what I'd just seen. She acted surprised and said that she hadn't the vaguest notion of what I was talking about. I took her by the arm and nearly dragged her to the computer and showed her the photo. She said, 'I have no idea where that fake picture came from, and I'm really pissed that you think that it's real! It's a fake, you damn fool!'

"I'm a damn fool? I was enraged, but she was so convincing that I didn't know what to think! Was it just my usual bad temper being jump-started? Am I insane to see what I saw and have her so hurt that I'd think it was her? Is she lying to me? Did someone fake her face and figure? I feel as if I'm going nuts."

My Response

"For the moment, let's assume, Brian, that your wife was actually on this dating site and had posted the photo. What then? Here are some of the possibilities: First, if she left this information on a clear site, she either expected and wanted you to see it, despite her denials, or it was an accidental or unconscious message. Second, your wife may be given to lies and deceit and cannot be trusted. Third, she may be searching for a real or fantastical relationship."

We discussed what Brian might have done had he carefully processed what he had seen to make sure of the facts before confronting his wife. We came up with the following list:

1. Print and copy the picture and all the pertinent information about the dating site.
2. Take the computer to an expert to check out the authenticity of the photo and the site.
3. Control your anger. To allay computer-related fears when there have been any suspicious happenings on a computer, check them out. The idea of talking to or confronting your partner about your questions is tempting but will not provide information. Only one person in a thousand guilty people is going to say, "Yes. I was interested in pornographic dating sites."
4. Do not confront your partner until you get information. This is very difficult advice to follow because you feel compelled to talk about your distress and you want your partner to know you are not stupid. If your wife tells you she is searching the Internet for a date, then what? Will you accept the admission that this is a truthful person who in some convoluted way is trying to maintain or leave the marriage?

"Although this sounds unlikely, an ugly Internet surprise can be the beginning of a new, interesting, exciting partnership. It can alert you to how much you really value your partner. People in relationships become sloppy in their treatment of each other. They disregard, demand, and disrespect their partners; they do not treat them like the friends they were during courtship. Too often, partners act as though a good relationship is their birthright and become angry if things do not go their way.

"It is difficult to think clearly when faced with the possibility that life as you knew it is about to change drastically. But there may be a positive outcome from this devastating revelation: if you thought that your relationship was in functioning order but it turns out to be moribund, you can ask yourself, do I really and truly want this marriage? What should I do to save it? Attacking the other person does not lead to revitalization of the partnership.

"I want you to consider the following: First, are you the best person you can be in this relationship? Second, has your temper eroded the commitment you made to be together? Third, anger is not your friend. Whether or not your bad moods contributed to the problem, you need to control your emotions. There are few realistic situations where anger is a repair mechanism. Fourth, do you understand that anger does not enhance communication, that it puts others down and shuts them out? Fifth, anger used as a management tool is a relationship spoiler."

Conclusion

Brian was a different person when his therapy concluded. In the past, he had avoided serious relationship discussions. Instead of talking with his wife about things that disturbed him and instead of listening to his wife's issues, Brian took opportunities to go into his "animal" mode: he would shout angrily, put his wife down with nasty comments, and stomp out of the house—and feel justified. In therapy, Brian agreed to give up his unproductive anger-related behavior. In fact, he said he was sorry and apologized to his wife. His wife remained adamant that she was innocent, and he realized she would never acknowledge any Internet indiscretion. He also was done with the idea that they could live happily ever after. Together, they decided the partnership was not doable because they were incompatible.

PART TWO

Passive, Passive/Aggressive, Impulsive, and Narcissistic Personality Disorders

art 1 detailed the difficulties encountered with angry partners who lashed out.

Personality disorders also arouse anger and interfere with healthy relationships. Partners of the person with a personality disorder may feel confused, angry, or frustrated but have difficulty ferreting out the exact problems because the partners with personality disorders, rather than act out, manipulate relationships under the radar of consciousness. To avoid confrontation, they unconsciously bury their thoughts and emotions and deflect or dance around conversations as if they are under siege. The other partner's direct communication—that is, the expression of his or her feelings and thoughts—is interpreted as a threat.

Living with a passive, passive-aggressive, impulsive, or narcissistic personality amounts to living in a hazy, frustrating, and anger-producing reality. Conflict becomes the bedrock of such relationships, and any attempts to solve the relevant problems are met with defensive behavior. Communication, meant to enlighten, is instead used by the defensive personality to direct a relentless and camouflaged rumble of palpable anger toward the other partner.

"What's wrong?" the recipient partner may ask.

The responses given by the defensive personality are often similar to the following:

- "No, I didn't say that."
- "I didn't do that."
- "That's not what I meant."
- "You're upsetting me."

The recipient partner—confused, unsure of what is real—can only watch as the relationship's life drowns in murky words and behavior, staring helplessly as the love boat drifts away.

CHAPTER 13
Passive Personality

Sasha: Emerging From A Lifetime Of Passivity

Being passive means to comply with orders, requests, or suggestions from others without actively responding or resisting. Passive pain is like a toothache that pushes on the nerve and never leaves; such pain shuts people down and drowns them in psychic pain, and they can only hope to learn to live with it. Without realizing it, these people put themselves in pain by carefully nurturing their fearful thoughts, which lock them in their passive stance.

In Sasha's case, she seemed to go along with her husband, no matter what the issue was. If something was okay with her husband, Matt, it was just fine with Sasha. She seemed to have no opinion of her own; however, she was filled with anger toward her husband's behavior.

Sasha was incapable of introspection or self-analysis. She was taken advantage of so often that she believed herself to be a martyr. Her sense of self-direction had been switched off. However, at a deeper level, she was in great distress and pain, and her passive defense system kept that pain from her consciousness.

Sasha and Matt had an unwritten marital contract: her role was to be the perfectly passive wife and content with her husband's decisions. Nothing was discussed seriously unless it was from Matt's understanding of the world. He made pronouncements, and if Sasha even hesitated or even seemed to question any proclamation, he got angry. Sasha went along—until Florida.

At age fifty-five, Matt decided that he'd had enough of his managerial position, that he was sick of the climate in Michigan, and that he needed to change his life and move to Florida. Sasha protested weakly, as usual. She was living in Florida before she realized it was time to seek help. When she called from Florida to make an appointment, she said, "Before I knew it, we were quickly packing up everything and were preparing to leave our children, grandchildren, friends, and family. We'll be in Michigan next month, and I want to stay in Michigan, but I need help."

In her first therapy session, Sasha, a fifty-four-year-old housewife, seemed to creep into my office. She was dowdy, wearing beige pants and a blouse and sneakers. She had no makeup, and her hair was brushed slightly. Right after she sat, tears immediately began to flow, and she started to softly express her powerful, negative feelings. "I hate Florida. When we settled in Florida, I realized I hated my husband. I feel as if I want to scream obscenities at him, which isn't like me at all. I can't stand the way he talks to me! He's always annoyed, snappy, and angry. He constantly barks at me and is adamant about his points of view."

"Is this new behavior?"

"No."

Sasha said she was depressed and blamed Matt, telling him he thought only of himself. She said Matt was shocked. "I always agreed with him and ignored his angry outbursts. He said he considered himself a considerate, loving husband and couldn't believe that I thought he was a tyrant." She smiled. "Boy, was he wrong!"

Trauma Produces Change

The traumatic move to Florida produced a crisis that Sasha could not ignore. In therapy, she examined herself and her life and found that she had a right to express her opinions and that she had a position. Expressing one of those opinions, she said, "I hate Florida, and I need to move back to Michigan."

Being a passive martyr—watching, waiting, and avoiding angry confrontations—no longer worked, thinking about action and taking action are two different things.

Sasha said, "Matt's anger still frightens me. I curl up inside and can't talk."

"It is difficult to reroute emotional responses," I said. "Although you aren't being harmed physically, you are being emotionally attacked. Your husband is a bully, and your fearful reactions encourage his behavior. The way you react makes him feel powerful.

"Speak your mind. Do not fall back into using the tentative and questioning talk of a little girl. You are a grown woman, take yourself seriously.

"Think about the following passive behaviors. Do they relate to you? If they do, how can they be altered?"

I gave her the following list of questions:

- Do you give up on directing your mind?
- Do you surrender to the moment?
- Do you dissociate or blank out?
- Do you think, "Oh no, I can't stand this!" but fearfully stay rooted to the spot?
- Do you feel that your partner is the king and that you are the helpless subject?
- Do you make excuses like "I have to go to the bathroom" or "I'm late" or "I have to get some sleep"?

"Begin a campaign with yourself. Instead of raising your defensive bar higher when your husband suggests that you are being defensive, acknowledge your defensiveness. Tell him that he is right; tell him what you are experiencing. You now know that you've spent your life being passive. It's important to be real and take responsibility for your passive style."

The Passive Style

"Living with a passive person is like living with a wet noodle," I said. "A passive person mentally slinks away from reality, acting like a coward. Passivity is a method of hiding yourself while you point the finger at your partner, either in your mind or in your behavior. You may say or think, 'There he goes again. He knows everything. I'm always wrong.' Or you, feeling disgusted, may move away and make sure your body language suggests censure. A disgusted look, shrug, tossing of the hair or the head, pursing lips, and rolling eyes—any of these quick responses indicate that you are dismayed or even appalled.

"Listen to yourself. You know when you are simply going along without verbalizing a point of view. Force yourself to state your position. What is the worst that can happen? Your husband may have a fit of anger, disagree, or discount your position. He may be verbally aggressive—but so what?

"If you want to stay stuck, that is okay, but be honest with yourself. You are getting something out of the present situation. By your acceptance, you let him know there is no reason for him to change."

Altering Behavior

Sasha and Matt worked on changing themselves, but they struggled. Matt came to therapy with Sasha. He believed she was having a midlife crisis; nevertheless, he was willing to work out their huge problem: where they were going to live. Sasha was adamant! She refused to fly back to Florida.

Eventually they decided to lease an apartment in Michigan for two years and keeps the house in Florida for the winter as an experiment. Sasha was satisfied, and Matt said he would fly back and forth if he needed the Florida environment. Their ability to work out a compromise indicated that a dramatic change had occurred—Sasha might have finally discarded her passive shell. However, slipping into past modes of thinking and behaving often happens. I thought it best to warn Sasha.

"Since you realize that falling into old behavior is natural, stay alert and vigilant. The minute you detect historical behaviors sliding into your life, stop, revisit your progress, and tell yourself not to flip back. You have left your cocoon, so stay out!"

Currently, Sasha and Matt are still working on their relationship, which is on an upward trajectory. In my opinion, their satisfaction is within reach, though they may experience a few bumps on the road in the near future.

While living with or being a passive person produces distress, there are other hidden defense mechanisms that result in mysterious and serious discontent. Chapter 14 describes how to define and deal with a passive-aggressive person.

CHAPTER 14
Passive/Aggressive Personality

*P*assive/aggressive is defined as "indirect resistance to the demands of others and avoidance of direct confrontation." Passive/aggressive individuals are afraid to express negative feelings directly; they are passive in their words and deeds. They listen, act as if they are in agreement, conveniently forget the issues or procrastinate, and then aggressively proceed to do whatever they want. The result is that their partners become frustrated and angry.

A seemingly passive person, Amber, often used passivity to exert indirect power: by being passive, she would indirectly become aggressive.

Tony, her husband, once said, "Honey, the movie [which Amber had agreed to see but did not want to attend] is starting at 8:15 p.m. We should leave at half past seven to avoid some traffic and get good seats."

"Sure," said Amber, "but first, I have to take a shower and get dressed... and prepare the kids' lunches."

Tony wanted to speed things up. "Honey, let's go—I'll do the kids' lunches. It's getting late."

When Tony suggested that time was running out, Amber slipped into using her passive/aggressive power. She used a few more gimmicks to make them late. "I can't leave until I find my lipstick," she said, causing the conversation to heat up. She positioned herself in the victim role by using such gimmicks. Continuing to stall, she said, "I'm going as fast as I can. You are making me nervous, and it's hard to get ready when I'm being attacked!"

They were late, and Tony eventually gave up on seeing the movie. The mission was now unconsciously accomplished: Tony's ox had been gored, and Amber, the passive/aggressive agent, could not be blamed.

Randy and Amanda

They were a perfectly balanced pair. Amanda was an accountant; Randy, a social worker. Amanda was orderly, conventional, and non-emotional, except when she became angry with Randy. Randy acted confused by Amanda's demands, made messes around the house, procrastinated, and forgot plans.

Randy and Amanda had been married for twenty-three years, and their kids were grown and living on their own. However, personality issues that had been on the periphery of their partnership had become intolerable. Still, both agreed they love each other and wanted to continue the marriage.

When Randy called for marriage counseling, he said, "We have already tried marriage counseling twice, so you could say we are jaded. We probably aren't good candidates for counseling, but we just don't know what else to do. We constantly butt heads and spend our days upset."

Often, people are not ready for emotional change. Their intellects tell them that their relationships are in shambles, but their emotions trail behind kicking and screaming, wanting to continue old behaviors. Some people become scared and desperately desire change because divorce is imminent. A third possibility is that others get so much satisfaction out of their difficulties that the misery becomes difficult to give up.

Marriage Counseling

Amanda, forty-seven, was dressed stylishly and impeccably. A tiny, five-foot dynamo, she was practically twitching in her eagerness to get the counseling show on the road. Randy was forty-six, talked slowly, and looked like Mr. Outdoors in his corduroy pants, boots, and plaid jacket.

With her eyes glued on me, Amanda said, "I get so tired of trying to talk to Randy. Half the time, he doesn't respond or just stares at me, or I catch him glancing at the newspaper or TV while I'm talking. And it's not as if I talk on and on. We barely have five minutes a day together. When I begin to get mad at him, I raise my voice." As she said this to me, she was actually raising her voice. "Then, of course, he won't talk to me. Or he will agree to do whatever I ask but then never follow through." She paused. "Well, that is just my perspective," she said, trying to soften the sound of her anger.

Randy's point of view was different. "I never seem to say the right thing. I know something is wrong with me when it comes to having serious talks with Mandy. I'm inept. Not only can't I carry on a conversation, but also I blank out. Both of those things drive her crazy.

"For example, last Tuesday, Mandy said she wanted to contact a couple we hadn't seen for a while and have them over. That was fine with me, but she got upset and angry with me because I didn't join in by planning the evening. When she gets upset like that, I feel myself shut down. I guess I zone out; I can't even hear her."

Amanda jumped in. "Instead of Randy saying something like, 'Sounds good' or 'No, I don't want to see them,' he just stares at me. I know I start pressing him. I feel as if I can't just go ahead and make plans without consulting him first, so when he acts as though he's not interested or seems to be out to lunch when I'm talking, I become upset. Sometimes he just decides to go to our cabin up north, and I'll be left holding the bag. He's done that before.

"I guess I don't do what I want. I keep waiting to see what he wants—but he never tells me. Or if we do plan something, he conveniently forgets! Randy often says he will do the things I ask him to do, like the chores around the house, and I always believe he means to take care of it, but I have to keep nagging him—even then I end up doing most things."

The Damaging Dance

Randy was put upon by Amanda's requests and claimed that he did not know how to communicate. He did know how to play the victim, a favorite role of passive/aggressive people, which made it seem that poor Randy was trying to do the best he could.

Randy passively played the "woe is me—my wife's words decide my feelings" card, but then he would proceed to do whatever he wanted to, whether he had indicated he was in agreement or not.

Amanda danced the passive/aggressive dance by making lots of reasonable suggestions and requests in a slightly agitated, plaintiff-like voice. She prepped herself to be angry, waiting for him to respond as he *should*, and then became furious when Randy retreated and failed to follow her lead.

They had danced this dance so many times before that they knew exactly how it would end, but to alter their words and behavior could be simple. Amanda could be definitive and simply say she was going to invite friends over, or Randy could indicate the plan was fine with him. Instead, they attended counseling, ignored suggestions, and refused to rewrite their individual histories, all the while pretending the situation was out of control.

Family-Inspired Neuroses

Amanda was the oldest child in her family. Her father was a mean-spirited, critical boss; her mother was indecisive, wimpy, and clingy. She identified with the aggressor, her father, and was the mouthy, active kid who fought with her father and whose mother could not mediate their disputes.

In most areas of her life, Amanda took charge. She chose a husband like her mother; however, she treated her husband as though he carried a whip as her father had done, expecting him to be the boss, despite her commitment to defy him subtly.

Randy, the oldest of five children, grew up in a family in which his father was gone most of the time, but when he was home, he was harsh and particularly punitive with Randy. Randy was no match for his father, so he adopted a policy of avoidance as his defense. When his father was home, Randy would stay in his room or leave the house and wander in the woods.

When his father criticized him, Randy would appear to listen and nod in agreement; then he would have his silent revenge by ignoring, delaying, and making errors. He used similar techniques with Amanda. Whenever she imploded or exploded, he would not respond, only disappear.

Such deeply embedded adaptations become neuroses; people carry them into adulthood and act them out in intimate relationships. (A *neurosis* is defined as "past adaptations that are dysfunctional when carried into adulthood.")

Caught in a knot of self-destructive behavior, Randy and Amanda were unable to see or appreciate how they had tied the knot of their problem. They believed the problem lay with the other and was rooted in external circumstances; thus, their interactions became a lethal form of self-sabotage.

Is There a Solution to these Reinforcing Negative Behaviors?

If Amanda were to understand her neurotic and unconscious contributions to their relationship, she could be clear with Randy about her expectations and grant him his right to conform or not. In that situation, they would understand the consequences if he exercised his options.

If Randy were to understand the origins of his avoidance and had the courage to let Amanda know what his preferences were while acknowledging her feelings at the same time, the hidden agenda would be interrupted.

They both had to take the chance of relating in unfamiliar but more effective ways if they were to find a way out of their unhappy communication failure.

Changing Patterns

How could Amanda develop new patterns that would be in harmony with her real needs? She would be served best if she understood what the psychological term *transference* meant. When a person unconsciously succumbs to transference, he or she applies historical personalities or prejudices to people or situations in the present.

All of us have been treated by someone else as if we *were* someone else. It is a common psychological occurrence. How many times have you protested that the other person is not responding to you as who you are? For example, someone close to you may say, "You're just like all the others!"

What others?

If you are a male, a woman may tell you that "you men are all alike!"

A friend may ask, "Why are you always trying to put me down!"

You probably protest to such comments and say they do not apply to you, and you will be right most of the time. You can only wonder whom you are standing in for.

For Amanda, Randy was a stand-in for her father, so she would interpret what he said, thought, and did *as if* he fit the mold of her father. She would repeatedly say or think, "You are just like my father," while ignoring who he actually was.

Randy, of course, had his own neurosis to deal with. People who intruded on his inner life or behavior must be like his perpetually dissatisfied, critical, and abusive father, so he regarded and avoided such people. Randy's fundamental defense was avoidance; therefore, he became elusive when Amanda treated him as if he were her father.

Unless both spouses understood the hidden agenda that powered their relationship, which was based upon past hurts and patterns, no amount of specific behavioral changes would result in a person-to-person relationship.

We humans cling to the known; we love our old thoughts as babies love their pacifiers. However, there is a time for babies to move on and give up those pacifiers, and there is a time for partners to move on to consciously rethinking their marriages.

Resolution

Amanda and Randy eventually recognized and admitted the neurotic foundation of their dance. A major step forward was their recognition that showing hostility to one another came from the past. They began to engage and assess thoughts that came to mind without distorting them with old templates. It was a long process, but the couple not only learned to slow down their automatic reactions but also learned to listen and respond to what the other person was actually intending.

This embracing of the true identities of each other did not mean that they walked into the sunset holding hands. They periodically fell back into old behaviors but became able to quickly reorient themselves, having learned how to recognize any slippage. Currently, they are more in contact with who they are individually and can more clearly assess each other; now they are able to relax and enjoy the virtues of their relationship and have celebrated their mutual escape from the realm of a passive/aggressive existence.

CHAPTER 15
Impulsive Personality

Impulsivity is defined as "acting on a whim without forethought or consideration of consequences." Impulsive individuals seem to lack prudence, the ability to plan, and the good sense to appreciate the effects their behavior has on others. Viewed as selfish, thoughtless, and even dangerous, impulsive people make decisions without hesitation and leave others to suffer the consequences.

Ashley and Keith's relationship shows how impulsive behavior can cause difficulties or exacerbate them.

The Problem

A premature return from a fun trip to Branson, Missouri, prompted Ashley to call my office and ask for an appointment. She wanted to meet me as soon as possible, at any time of day or night. When we met two days later, she explained that her trip had ended in a marital emergency.

Ashley was thirty-two years old, slim, well dressed, and calm. She sat up straight, with her hands folded, and said, "I took an early flight back, alone, after Keith and I had an argument. Keith's my husband.

"It was awful. He embarrassed me, yelled, and stomped out in front of a roomful of people, and he wouldn't tell me what the problem was.

In fact, it has been five days, and he's still not talking. He knows that drives me crazy."

Leaning forward, Ashley said, "You won't believe what started it all. It was my cousin's husband who told me why Keith was mad. We were all at a Western country bar when my husband asked me to dance. I said no because the music sounded like a square dance. That's it! That's why he won't speak."

Crossing her legs and relaxing, she said, "Actually, that is how he is—he will just act on a whim. Two months ago, he bought a very expensive new truck, even though he has a truck that is only a year old. Keith never mentioned to me that he was even thinking of a new truck, and then he came up with some ridiculous excuse for buying it. I am so upset when he does these things. I'm just flabbergasted because we've talked about being open with one another, especially about money, but when he wants something or feels something—bingo!—there isn't any conversation. He just does what he wants to do.

"He's not a total jerk. In his defense, I do have to say he's a wonderful father to Ryan, our eight-year-old son, but it seems as if he has all the power. Like now, he's not speaking to me. He's the one who's wrong, and I'm the one who suffers."

I asked, "Were there any difficulties between you and your husband before you left home?"

"No, everything was fine."

Everything was *not* fine. As it turned out, Keith's sister, who was having money problems, invited herself to Branson, and off the top of his head, Keith said sure. His sister not only came with them but also stayed in their hotel room to save money, and Ashley spent much of the vacation with her.

"Is it possible your husband felt left out or jealous?"

"Yes, I think he was, but he shouldn't have been. I didn't dance with anyone, except his sister—plus, the invitation was his idea!"

The Branson episode was an issue that implied a deeper problem.

Ashley's History

In later therapy sessions, Ashley revealed that she grew up in a careful, perhaps fearful, environment, where comfort for the family meant doing the right thing: frugality, diligence, time management, and a strict moral and ethical code. Responsibility was the rule they lived by.

Ashley had already made one move that shook the family: she got divorced. Given her conservative family, divorce was a brave step. She said her parents were so upset by the idea of divorce that they went through hers in worse emotional shape than she did.

According to Ashley, her previous marriage was with a calculating, stingy, controlling man who overanalyzed every decision, no matter the size. Her subsequent marital choice—Keith, an impulsive free spirit—implied that she went to the other extreme in hopes of disentangling herself from her family's and first husband's restrictions.

The first and second husbands, while seemingly different, allowed Ashley to play the victim, which covered up her own thoughtlessness.

Basic Conflict

Ashley was conflicted. Although her husband often told her that he loved her and valued the marriage, he would shrug and dismiss her problems with his impulsive behavior.

Keith was not compelled to live by society's standards. He acted on his whims and spoke without thinking. He was a person with boundary problems, a trait Ashley unconsciously admired. At the same time, his behavior raised her anxiety and infuriated her, and she could not help living out her "do the right thing" training by struggling with him. Ashley became vigilant, wary, and fearful of his next inappropriate remark or behavior and caused herself further grief by angrily trying to help him understand why he needed to reform.

"Your husband is driven by his impulsive nature," I said. "Unless he becomes consistently upset by his own behavior, change is not in his future. If you are interested in improving and continuing your marriage, give up the idea of altering his basic personality. Instead, it's up to you to alter your behavior."

"He's the one who's impulsive. I don't understand. Why should I change?"

"Why should you be the one putting forth all the effort when he is the culprit? This is *your* life. This is *your* husband. If you prefer a happy life with Keith, you need to be the one who gets the ball rolling. When you learn to act differently, he will respond differently. Your serious efforts to understand and change the status quo will reap huge rewards, particularly since Keith has declared his desire to please you."

In a therapy session several weeks later, Ashley was sitting primly, with her hands folded in her lap. She said, "We're finally talking, thanks to you. I told him I was sorry I ignored him in Branson; I took responsibility for that. But I am still mad he wouldn't talk to me. I have to gag myself or go into another room so that I don't blow up and tell him what a jerk he was."

"Were you sincere when you took responsibility for your behavior?" I asked.

"In a way, I was, but I wanted him to say he was sorry too."

"You've grown up believing that you and your family know how to talk and act properly, which gives you the sense that you are in a position of authority. You assess others according to your standards and stamp 'I'm right—you're wrong' in your brain. Those standards may be right for you but do not necessarily suit everyone else, including your husband."

Solutions
"Do not dramatically react to his words and behavior by chastising and showing disapproval. Do not say or ask anything that resembles the following comments."

I gave her the following list:

- Why did you say that?
- What's wrong with you?
- How many times have we discussed your impulsive actions?
- You act like a child and do whatever you want.
- Why do you hurt my feelings by not talking to me before you act?

"Or you indicate your disapproval by using negative body language, such as giving him disgusted looks or physically turning away. Or you shut down mentally.

"Be as understanding to Keith as you would be to a stranger. Rather than treat him with outrage, indicate that you are puzzled, surprised, and even curious about his impulsive behavior. Then—and this is important— be patient and quiet and let him talk.

"The next suggestion is difficult and will not seem like a solution. It will be difficult to put into operation because you have other negative emotional thoughts about him, and you feel he should know those thoughts. If you verbalize them, he will respond by turning away, and his feelings would be hurt. Or he might angrily attack you and your lack of understanding.

"Instead, work on your own train of thought. Begin by practicing the law of substitution. For each thought that feeds you the idea that your husband should not act in particular ways, substitute a positive idea, such as 'I love Keith,' 'I am interested in how his mind works,' 'Keith has wonderful attributes,' 'Keith is a good father,' or 'Keith is a good provider.'

"Another thing you could do is write down your difficulties with him, hold the problems up to the light of reason, dissect them, and mull them over. Then cut up the paper, burn it, put it in the garbage, and throw it away.

"When you think, 'This will not work,' use powerful, emotional words to inform your mind that negative reactions have not made a difference. When you talk to yourself, call up powerful feelings to make the point. I know it sounds like hocus-pocus, but if you do not make a conscious, powerful statement to your brain, the dialogue will simply be a part of the sixty thousand thoughts that roam daily through your mind.

"Through these actions, you will change the neurons in your brain. To alter neurons, you must monitor and discard old thoughts by catching reactions and muffling habitual words.

"The trick is to keep your resolve. Ideas, as you know, have a way of slipping away. Writing helps cement ideas in your mind. You will need sticky notes, or leave messages in your planner, on your computer, or in your cell phone. Mainly, you need the message to stick firmly in your brain.

"If your husband uses his silent tactic, react to his silence with silence. Again, as difficult as it is, keep your mouth shut, and let your bubbling anger go. View his silence as his tactic to control himself *and* you.

"When a moratorium is declared, the silence will be over and the time will be right to discuss with empathy your reaction to his withdrawal. Tell him that you understand his need to keep himself under control but that you, of course, cannot read his mind and want to know his thoughts.

"If he refuses to talk, simply say you will talk about it another day— and three days later, talk again. Do not be discouraged if that does not work; three days later, bring up his silence again. You must talk with understanding. Don't use anger or make snide comments; don't provide some historical overview.

"Keith is impulsive. At the same time, he wants to please you, and I believe his impulsivity is also a problem to him, because you have told me he is defensive (especially in regard to money), backtracks, or plays the you-do-it-too card. That is, he'll tell you that 'you buy clothes' or 'you go on vacations' with a negative tone.

"You chose an impulsive partner for good reason. You may think, 'I did not know he was this impulsive when I fell in love,' but that makes no difference now.

"It is important for you to recognize that impulsiveness is a feature of his personality. Your unhappiness will not make it go away, nor will it help him work on control; instead, your husband will become defensive when you respond by chastising him.

"The overview of the relationship is that you and Keith are at opposite ends of a pole: you are conservative; he is liberal. Either you can use those contrasting qualities to balance the relationship, or you can nervously watch and wait for his next moves. In the latter path, you will become a reactor rather than an actor in your own life.

"Being an actor requires that you choose your thoughts because they direct your life. You will be vigilant—that quality is a part of you—but at the same time, you must think ahead. Think about his excellent qualities, such as why you love him, and when a distracting impulse occurs, think of effective responses. Get rid of thoughts like 'He should not act that way,' 'He shouldn't say those things,' and 'He's making me mad.'

"You do not add happiness to your life when you allow yourself negative ideas. You will feel happy when you use your mind in positive ways to solve problems.

Information for Keith

"As an impulsive person, you think quickly and act quickly. If a thought comes to mind, you immediately say or act out the thought. The problems are that anxiety is only temporarily relieved and your relationship takes another hit.

"When you impulsively react, say things like, 'Oops, sorry, I didn't mean to say that,' but trying to back track won't fly indefinitely. Or you may not be sorry. You gain pleasure from acting impulsively or with a mean spirit.

"Tension makes it difficult for you to go beyond your experience and be empathic. You are often flooded with powerful, overwhelming thoughts that must be put into action. You have a reputation; everyone knows how you are. Words just pop out. What can you do? You are the victim of your mind.

"On the contrary, your actions and reactions are voluntary. You cause your relationship trouble whenever you do or say anything that comes to mind. Because a thought came to mind does not mean it has merit.

"Your anxiety, which is based in fear, underlies your impulsive thought processes. To capture your own attention and to take charge of impulsive behavior increase anxiety, so it is difficult to stop and think, 'These thoughts and their consequent behavior don't work. I think I'll stop this.'

"An impulsive action pays off momentarily because your tension decreases and you feel powerful. However, the powerful feeling does not last long because you are quickly forced to defend your position to your partner, who has become angry and has backed away.

"The following questions and comments are to help you gain insight and recognize impulsive thoughts and action."

- Do quick reactions express real thoughts and feelings?
- Do you have to back pedal or apologize after you act?
- You have to say what you are thinking or you cannot stand the tension.
- You are so caught up in your need to speak that your partner's point of view disappears.

"The ability to look into the self is not a God-given right. Few people are blessed with self-insight. However, you do know if you are getting what you want in your relationship and whether you are pleased with your actions and communication style."

Positive Outcome

Ashley and Keith continue to struggle but are willing to admit their errors. They focus on using comments like "oops, here's what I meant to say" and "sorry, let's start over." Essentially, they are trying to turn potentially damaging accusations or unnecessary comments into positive moments for their relationship. Their goals are to stand guard by using mindfulness and to eliminate anger, blame, and punishing silence.

Their relationship is moving in a positive direction because they are accentuating the positive and eliminating the negative.

CHAPTER 16
Passive and Passive/Aggressive Personalities

Lisa and Eric

Lisa reported that she had finally had enough. On the phone, she said, "I think the marriage is really over, but I want to check out all options."

Lisa came to my office January 2, right after the holidays. Her daughters and their families had flown from other states for Christmas, and the normal chaos ensued with all the kids and extra people.

Lisa said, "I thought everything was okay. I didn't notice any hostility but my daughters were so uncomfortable with my husband's behavior that they changed their airline tickets in spite of the fact that they were slapped with significant penalties."

As Lisa talked about her girls' leaving, she kept rubbing her eyes and fidgeting with a Kleenex. "My children have never liked my husband and vice versa. Eric is a know-it-all. He doesn't initiate conversation or indicate any interest in my kids' lives, but he butts in when they talk, makes snide comments, and tells them what they should have done or should do in the future. He can't shut up. After the fact, if he has said something inappropriate and I point it out, he just can't see it and says I'm being a bitch.

"Eric also has a way of ending conversations. He dogs us. When I want to have private conversations with the girls—conversations that have nothing to do with him—there he is. He insinuates himself into every conversation and even follows us into the bedroom.

" I talked to Eric and explained nicely that I have few opportunities to be with them and asked him to please cut us some slack. He was insulted and angry. He said, 'What did I do? I just want to be part of the family.'"

Lisa put down her tissue and seemed to relax. "Eric does not have a clue that his behavior is a problem or pretends he doesn't have a clue—I don't know which because he is very intelligent.

"He sits around, takes everything in, and then jumps in with nasty words and acts innocent. Or he might leave randomly. There were times when everyone was chatting together and he stood up and left in a grumpy manner.

"Most of the time, I can manage him when we're alone, but that is really what I do—I *manage* him.

"What do you mean by 'manage him'?" I asked.

"For two weeks, sometimes three weeks, he might be quiet and into himself; however, he makes cranky comments regularly, probably daily. I'm so used to his talk I don't even hear it. At least that's what my girls say.

"Then out of the blue, he will start up again. If I ask him to do something around the house, he will say that if I weren't such a rotten housekeeper, he wouldn't have to be put to so much trouble. I usually ignore those comments because they are just silly; the truth is we have an immaculate house.

"He often says that my spending is out of control, which is ridiculous because I'm a miser compared with him. Eric makes huge bonuses every year. We have company stock and other stock.

"In other words, he just says and does anything that pops into his mind. He often gets upset over things that are not his ideas, and when he does, he becomes a verbal maniac. He will become angry, put me down, charge out of the house without saying anything, go to the store, come back with stuff we don't need, and then resume attacking me.

"Eric never acknowledges that what he has said or done is wrong, and he definitely never admits that his behavior is inappropriate. However, he will be quiet and contrite for a few days after these episodes. I've always accepted his quiet behavior as a type of apology. I believe that these highs and lows are just a part of his personality.

"Now, since my kids are unwilling to put up with him, I really feel torn and want to do something about my situation. What should I do?"

"Good question. What do you want to do?" I asked.

Lisa was blank. "I'm not sure."

Lisa and Eric's coupling was passive and aggressive. Evidently, the two of them knew their roles, and without interruption, their passive and aggressive roles continued unabated, regardless of their houseguests' observations.

To interrupt this perfect fit would be difficult unless Lisa was dedicated to change and able to follow through. From her story, it seemed that either she was seeking therapy because she was able to see herself through her daughters' eyes, or she was calling for counseling to appease her daughters, to let them know she was doing something.

"Have you asked your husband to join you in therapy?"

"No."

"Why not?"

"It would be a disaster. He would be furious if he knew I was talking to you."

"What is the worst thing that happens when he's angry?"

"Oh, he won't hit me or anything, but I like peace. I can't stand all that tension."

"Avoidance makes emotionally aggressive situations worse. You are predicting an emotional disaster for yourself, frightening yourself. When you magnify the situation, it ramps up fear and, in fact, floods your mind with anxiety. Your heart pounds and rational thinking disappears, and you reinforce exactly what is scaring you. Is that true?"

Lisa agreed. "Yes. I can actually feel my heart beating. It feels like a heart attack."

"I know it's very uncomfortable to confront yourself and to take a different stance with your husband. Start with a baby step by talking to yourself—whether he is in the room and carrying on or whether you are alone with your thoughts.

"Say to yourself, 'Calm down—I know exactly how he will react. I've seen it before. He's like a little kid having a temper tantrum. He will get over it. It will not be a calamity; life will go on. So what if he's angry?' Could you do that?"

"It's weird, but I'm afraid of him. It scares me to think of saying anything to him when he's angry...I could try."

A confident-looking Lisa arrived at my office the next week and said, "I just kept saying the words you told me to say to myself over and over, on the way home from the office and at home. Eric asked me what was wrong; he could probably tell I was preoccupied. I went straight to my computer and wrote out your ideas. Even when I went to bed, I talked to myself. It worked!

"I feel stupid saying this, but I was brave enough to ask him about counseling and felt calm while asking him! He said absolutely not. He said he does not need counseling, that only I do. That made me smile— to myself, of course."

Lisa's self-dialogue illustrated the power of changing thoughts. Unless Eric experienced his behavior as dystonic, there would be no reason for him to change. His behavior relieved his tension and gave him an added bonus: power over Lisa.

Using anger as a defensive maneuver to manage one's self and others works in the short term but is destructive as a way of life. Partners either succumb, like a beaten puppy, or take charge of themselves (as Lisa did) and look for solutions.

Lisa's commitment to therapy and positive change will make or break the marriage because therapy will be a threat to Eric. He prefers the status quo, and he will definitely work to make sure Lisa gives up treatment.

CHAPTER 17
Narcissistic Personality

Falling in love with a narcissist is easy. Narcissists are seductive, charming, and solicitous, and they focus on what they want; if it happens to be you—watch out!—you are about to find out that you have a tiger by the tail, a tiger that will turn around, bite you, and make you conform to their desires. If you do not, your life will be miserable. Unfortunately, an authentic narcissistic does not reveal his or her true identity until the targeted person is safely trapped in some way. The target can be a spouse, child, employee, or anyone in a close relationship.

Narcissists have room for one personality—their own. Living with a narcissist means jumping into his or her self-adoration, grandiosity, and feelings of entitlement, and the target must live life through the narcissist's eyes only. If you do not fall into step with a narcissist's self-love, you will be demeaned, ignored, and criticized; you will become a victim of the narcissist's lack of empathy. Your thoughts and feelings are of no importance.

If these qualities sound like a relationship nightmare, they are. This array of attributes paints a repelling picture of in-house character traits that are private and remain hidden until a target is firmly ensconced in the narcissist's lair. In general, the public life of a couple with one narcissist is usually nothing more than a charming social performance, as the following couple will show.

Brittany

Brittany used a narcissistic method to leave her marital relationship. She was forty years old. She was slim and beautiful and tall and had black hair and dark eyes. As she explained her situation to me, she smoothed her hair back and spoke with a definitive, dramatic style.

Brittany and Michael, her husband, and I had marched through many months of marriage counseling four years ago, yet she talked as if we had seen each other yesterday.

"I can't be me! All I am is a work drudge; my personality is gone. I'm a blank. I take care of others, and no one cares or appreciates what I do. Can't you see I've lost myself?

"I am not an *I*. I am a compilation of other people who need me to take care of them. I have been in the mom role for so long that Brittany has disappeared. I have no idea who I am, and now that I know that I am a nobody, I can't stop thinking and worrying about that realization. If I've been a nobody all along but only now realize it, why should I care?"

She paused and looked up at me as if she were a child. "I've told Michael I need time to find myself because the way I feel is preventing me from being a good wife and mother. I know my unhappiness is taking a toll on the children. You know how sensitive children are. They are always asking, 'What's wrong, Mommy?' What can I say? 'I hate being here'?"

Moving forward to the edge of my office couch, sitting stiff with a rigid spine, Brittany said, "I want my husband to move out, to leave. I need time to find myself; I don't need to worry about his coming and going. He travels all the time. When he's home, I am agitated; just his being around makes me angry."

"What about your husband makes you angry?"

Brittany waved a hand. "Everything. For example, I have some male friends who come to visit from Canada. Michael gets all excited when they stay here if he's out of town. He knows who they are—he's met them. I really get mad when he complains. I'm entitled to have friends. I won't stop having friends here just because he is acting like a baby!"

"Your husband tells you he is disturbed. Your children have heard their father's anxiety, and they must be confused. It is inappropriate for a woman alone to have men in the house overnight, even though they're friends."

"Not for me," she said in an edgy, huffy tone. "My children know my friends and like them." She tried to put an end to my message. "I have a plan, but I need you to back me up; otherwise, I know Michael won't go for it. I am going to suggest we rent an apartment for him or he can stay with his brother until I get myself together. I doubt he will find that an attractive option, but I need to be away from him for a while. After six months or a year, if we have established a better relationship, then we can start again on a happier note. That's my proposal."

"It sounds as if you are ready to separate, but your husband has no idea what's on your mind. It would be helpful to the family to talk this situation out, to help your husband understand how you feel, and to develop a plan together."

"No, I can't talk to him; we just can't talk together."

"Brittany, help me understand your anger and why you are eager to remove him from the house."

She skipped past my question and said, "My plan will work if Michael is reasonable, which he probably won't be, and that makes me angry—that's all. I came to counseling just to tell you what's going on with me, but I do not need therapy. Michael does."

Brittany had solved her problem. She was done with the marriage and was handing her husband over to me to manage the fallout.

Michael

Michael, forty-two, came to therapy a few days later, looking disheveled. He could not believe Brittany's attitude; he was in shock. "For my wife to tell me out of the blue that she wants a separation is just...I can't believe she is serious. She won't have anything to do with me. If she lowers herself to talk to me, she hisses and practically spits words at me. I don't get it. I don't know why she's mad.

"I travel a lot for business, and my work is why we have our nice home, all the extra things for the kids, nice cars, and so forth. I thought that providing was my main job. Why is she doing this? She says she has to find herself. Why does she have to separate to find herself?"

"Michael, you are in my office to understand how to proceed. Is that correct?"

"Yes."

"You can't change anything at this moment, but with information, you will calm down. Right now, I want you to take three deep breaths and to tell yourself to relax. Can you do that?"

"Yes, I will...but I can't sleep. I can't eat. My mind is going in circles. Sometimes I feel furious, but I don't dare express those feelings. She puts me down in front of the kids, and then I get defensive and upset. We fight, and I'm the goat. I'm living a nightmare. I pray that I'll wake up and everything will be normal.

"Brittany says terrible things to and about me when the kids are present. For example, right in front of them, she accused me of having an affair, which is not true. She also said, 'You want to leave the kids and me without money or a place to live.' All I could say at the time was 'That's not true,' which sounded lame. She says these things with a weepy, teary voice while she huddles with the kids and sneers at me over their heads.

"I'm pretty sure the kids believe her because they say, 'Daddy, we need money,' and other similar stuff. It makes me sick."

He ignored the tears rolling down his cheeks. I handed him a Kleenex box, and he blew his nose before he continued. "Brittany will scream at me, tell me I'm not a man, and ask why don't I take charge. She just acts crazy, but when her cell rings, she will stop in the middle of a scream and talk in a friendly voice. After she hangs up, she will start screaming again.

"What do you think? Will she get over this? I don't know what to do, and she won't tell me what to do, except say I should leave. I love her, and I can't lose my family. So how can I solve a problem that doesn't make sense?"

In their relationship, serious marital issues had been brewing long before Michael's sudden traumatic experience of being rejected. On work assignment for two weeks at a time, he had been in a relationship fog, ignoring their problems. Weekend disagreements and lack of intimacy would disappear whenever he flew away, and he would find relief when he focused on his career.

As children, we are seldom taught problem-solving skills for relationships, and we do not observe parents who discuss differences intelligently and reach satisfactory solutions, particularly when emotions are the core problem. Michael's original home was a controlled environment in which emotions were not tolerated. "Get over it," "Don't be a crybaby," "What are you, a sissy?"—These were the messages Michael heard when he was a child. Now, he could not "get over it" and calm down—the emotional fireworks in his brain were out of control.

Michael's History

Michael's parents married and left Germany to join their siblings in the United States, as well as to establish themselves as US citizens. Michael's mother ruled their home with an iron fist. Life was simple, and the rules were the rules. If Michael stepped out of line, there would be serious consequences. Relationship issues and feelings were unimportant. The family's goal was to create a better life through hard work, by quietly fitting in, and by establishing expectations that the children should conduct themselves properly.

When Michael was an adult with a family of his own, he understood that his job was to financially care for his family, just as his father had done, and his wife was supposed to be the one who ran the household.

He was emotionally unprepared for his marriage crisis.

Brittany's History

Brittany was a narcissist formed by a mother who was also a narcissist. Mothering requires that positive attention be given to a child, for children mirror their parents' behavior. Ideally Mothers say things like "what a good girl! You ate all your breakfast" or "thank you for helping Mommy." Since narcissists are interested only in themselves, children become an impediment, a bother; they are ignored and put down. Narcissists are unable to recognize and assist children's development; rather, they impede children's self-growth and understanding.

Brittany had attachment issues. She grew up insecure and with self-loathing; she believed that her mother had not loved her. One of the many things Brittany's mother told her was that she never wanted children, especially a child like Brittany. Brittany tried to be perfect to please her mother, but she could never do anything right.

As a narcissist, Brittany took care of herself by being a star and seeking positive attention. Words that enhanced her position, whether fact or fiction, were stated with a sense of reality. Without empathy, bubbling with inner rage, she would cut family members to the bone with anger, sarcasm, and hurtful comments.

Assessment

Until a crisis occurs, partners in a relationship usually tune each other out. Brittany and Michael would nod and appear to listen, but they both had difficulty in actually hearing and taking each other's words and feelings seriously. Brittany had finally gotten Michael's attention, and his auditory system was on high alert. He was no longer lounging through weekends or focusing on his work and travel schedule. Michael was in turmoil; confused and crazed, he could not think straight.

These two had been on a parallel path, marching together while their minds and emotions were elsewhere. Michael explained away Brittany's explosive temper as "her dramatic style." The idea that Michael must leave so that Brittany could be herself sounded ludicrous to Michael because he was certain that theirs had been a happy marriage. He believed he had done everything he could to make her happy. As far as he was concerned, the marriage had not changed.

In our previous counseling sessions, Brittany claimed that her demands had to be met, or the marital relationship would end—it was her way or the highway. At that time, the problem for Brittany was Michael's father. Brittany refused to speak with him and insisted that Michael do the same, which is a common alienation tactic used by narcissists—that is, eliminate the rivals. A compromise and temporary peace was achieved through combined family-therapy meetings, and I say *temporary* because trouble is always on the horizon with a narcissist.

Immediate Problem

Brittany had a plan to rid herself of Michael and alienate the children from their father. She chose a victim stance to put herself in the right and reduce her husband to emotional rubble with drummed-up, manipulative words and pretended anger.

I told Michael to follow a particular action plan: "When Brittany verbally attacks you, do not jump in and argue, defending yourself only exacerbates the problem. Take charge of yourself; tell yourself to calm down over and over, if necessary.

"Acknowledge Brittany's words by saying you feel sorry for how she feels. Then, and although this is *very* difficult, steel yourself when she talks—again, stay calm and in command of yourself. Say things like, 'Brittany, that is not true. Those words are abusive. They hurt my feelings and upset the children.' Then walk to the other room. You cannot win when you are faced with a person who will say anything to hurt and disparage you in front of your children.

"When the children are present, indicate that her words about you are not true; then leave the room. Whether the children are present or not, do not return anger with anger, and absolutely do not join in by maligning her character. Above all, do not defend yourself. Why should you defend yourself if what she is saying is false?

"If Brittany follows you to the other room to continue her angry tirade, ask the children if they want to go outside, take a walk, ride bikes, or go for ice cream. It is imperative that you remove the children, if you can. If Brittany attempts to physically detain them, do whatever you can to calm the situation. Do not ramp up your own agitated feelings.

"Concentrate on the best interest of the children. Children become frightened when parents are out of control. Angry, mean parents teach their children that these behavior should be used to solve relationship problems and that they should try to out-scream and out-fox others. Parents acting on their anger only provide a negative-learning model for their children. Your calm control will help them understand that they have other options."

Long-Term Solution

Individuals who are divorcing or separating do not have to slice and dice the other person. To do so in front of children indicates zero empathy and care about the children's well being.

"Michael, do not grapple with her ideas or talk about what is real or what she should do. Brittany is at war with you, and she does not care what you think or care who is harmed. In fact, she wants to bring you down and ruin the children's relationship with you.

"You are the steady, stable parent, and you must remain so when you do not rise to her bait. Keep calm and cool!

"For the benefit of the children, describe what she is doing. Every time she starts her hysterical rambles, explain that her words are mean spirited and overly emotional and that she is out of control. Then leave the room. Blow-by-blow tactics will not accomplish anything.

"Brittany wants you gone and is being persistent and consistent with that message. If she remains adamant, a divorce will be on the horizon. It is time to grasp that message, see an attorney, and explore your rights.

"Keep in mind that the divorce process may be advantageous since custody issues often involve court-ordered psychological evaluations."

Conclusion

It took Michael weeks to calm himself and gain control, but he was finally successful. He also began a divorce process. When it was appropriate, he rented a home nearby and, through the court system, set up a timetable to share custody of the children. Michael was prepared to battle for the children, but Brittany did not engage in a custody battle. Michael suspected that she was spending time with her friends.

Currently, Michael calls my office occasionally to touch base and let me know how he and the children are progressing. Life is relatively calm, although Brittany tries to interfere with his fathering by failing to follow the scheduled timetable arrangements for the children. Overall, he feels that his family is doing well.

Rigid Defenses Do Not Bring Happiness

These four personality disorders—impulsiveness, passiveness, passive/aggressiveness, and narcissism—are unconscious and habit driven.

The paradox in attending to thoughts and focusing on developing desirable conscious thought processes is that people with personality disorders have automatic thoughts; the ability to see and hear thoughts from another person's standpoint or their own is usually unavailable.

But there is wiggle room in any personality disorder—some personality disorders are unable to change, they are written in stone, while others have moderate relationship flexibility. Given the facts of personality disorders, it is up to you to decide if or how you are going to proceed with your relationship: will you continue to struggle, change your mindset, find a comfortable solution and accept the facts, or leave?

Living with a personality disorder is a possible explanation for why you are confused, frustrated, and angry. Another explanation is detailed in part 3. Negative habits of mind generated by our original families, genetic programming, or low self-esteem are projected onto others through relationship language. These communication habits disrupt instead of connecting partners.

PART THREE
Criticism, Contempt, Sarcasm, And Silence

Communication Patterns

Communication is a barometer of relationship status. Good communication is easily defined: a person is open and direct about his or her thoughts and feelings; he or she listens and tries to understand what others are thinking and feeling.

Positive words, tones of voice, and body language flow when there is a meeting of the minds. Another person's remarks are respected and acknowledged, whether the ideas are similar or different.

Difficult communication includes the refusal to listen to others and denial that another person's suggestions, ideas, or feelings are valid.

Troubled talk is argumentative and contradictory, indicating a lack of interest in or rejection of the other person's feelings, actions, or point of view. Negative emotions are aroused when communication is riddled with criticism, sarcasm, or contempt. Troubled talk generates anger, frustration, and disrespect. A free and smooth-flowing interaction is no longer possible because neither party can relax; in this situation, a casual remark can turn into an explosive, negative experience.

Because we are social animals, we need to talk. Our happiness, moods, and capacity to flourish are enormously influenced by interactions with others as well as our own self-dialogue. When a partner refuses to speak or if dialogue is laced with complaints, criticism, or sarcasm, communication runs into a dead end.

Behavior and words constitute communication and can block a relationship's connections. Ask yourself if you do any of the following:

- Deliberately push buttons—that is, poke at your partner's vulnerable areas
- Act innocent, stare blankly, or say nothing when you know what's going on
- Divert attention
- Downplay emotions
- Act emotionless or flatlined

If you participate in any of the above behaviors, do not excuse yourself. Instead, acknowledge and alter your bad behavior. Your words and behavior are a defense of pretense; you know you are acting, and your partner knows it too.

Short-Circuiting Communication

The following communication confusers are muddy and indirect discussion closures and generally fly under the radar of criticism. Each method either borders on criticism or presents flat-out disapproval.

- Right: your partner knows the answer but disregards your point of view.
- Defensive: your partner cannot take responsibility for his or her actions. You are wrong.
- Expert: your partner solves your problem whether you want him or her to or not.

- Silent: because you disagree, your partner will not talk.
- Martyr: your partner immediately and dramatically becomes the victim.
- Stoic: your partner responds to feelings with disdain.
- Harps: your partner nags.
- History buff: your partner brings up every past hurt.

Once you recognize the communication styles, you gain the opportunity to examine your reactions and respond differently. Your job with others is not to point out their communication shortcomings but to consider that their styles are written in stone, so you should alter your thinking and respond differently.

Criticism, Sarcasm, Contempt, and Silence

Your partner refuses to listen to you or share feelings. Argumentative and defensive, he or she insists that his or her thoughts and feelings are all that count, dismissing and diminishing your ideas with criticism, sarcasm, or contempt, inflaming or dead-ending conversations.

Or, rather than being direct, your partner passively acts out negativity that is apparent in facial expressions and body language, such as shrugging shoulders, rolling eyes, or making dismissive hand movements. When asked what these gestures mean, your partner acts surprised or pretends to be innocent or is silent.

You are familiar with body language. Even a stranger's face portrays basic, universal emotional codes recognized across all cultures. Sadness, anger, fear, disgust, embarrassment, joy, and happiness belong to an emotional book that anyone can open.

In an intimate relationship, your partner not only opens the book but also reads it. Your face, voice, and body language present your partner with an emotional map, and under the best circumstances, that map leads to empathy and understanding. When, instead of understanding, your partner is silent or body language is used to convey criticism, sarcasm, or contempt, distrust and confusion reign.

CHAPTER 18
Criticism

How To Think About And Handle Criticism

If you are the victim of criticism, the temptation is to insist that your partner stop attacking you. When your verbal reactions to his or her criticisms do not change your partner's critical patterns the first twenty times, either this person is choosing to play deaf, or their unconscious brain grid will not allow a docking neuron. Either way, your words fall on deaf ears.

You are in charge when you accept facts. Your partner is critical. It is up to you to alter your behavior.

Jackie and Doug

The critic's communication habit can include a quick put down or a disturbing, incessant commentary about you, the imperfect partner. Jackie and Doug's relationship provides an example of criticism that gained momentum through the years and was the hallmark of their relationship.

During their twelve years together, Jackie and Doug gradually picked up their critical pace with one another until life became a battleground. They came to marriage counseling as a last resort, hoping to decide whether to continue their marriage.

Doug, thirty-six at the time, was a sales rep. He was casually well dressed, a quick-thinking talker, and used to getting his way. At home, he needed things to be clean and orderly.

Jackie, thirty-four, was an occasional dress designer, but she spent most of her time at home with their two preschool children. She was slender and very pretty. She had curly black hair and blue eyes and a lot to say, particularly about her perceived shortcomings.

In their first therapy session together, Jackie began by sitting up straight and keeping her head up while putting herself down. "I know my own faults, at least," she said, glancing at Doug. "I'm scatterbrained. I go from one thing to another without finishing anything. On some days, I clean; on other days, I don't. I yell at the kids incessantly one day, and then I'm patient on the next. My behavior drives Doug up the wall. I hate the end of the day when he comes home, because I know he's going to walk in, point out something I didn't do, get mad, and call me names. He's very critical of me."

Doug stared at Jackie during her discourse as if he was slightly amused but puzzled by her talk. "Of course I'm disturbed when I get home and find the house as messy as it was the day before and the kids skidding around the house and yelling. It's chaos.

"Frankly, I think Jackie is depressed and needs medication. She is scattered. She has never been able to figure out how to clean the house, which is such a simple thing." He looked at me for confirmation. "Anyone can clean a house. House cleaners are paid minimum wage, yet she is confounded by any household task. She's not stupid."

"Well," said Jackie, interrupting him, "I don't criticize you daily."

"No, just every other day."

Jackie continued, crying and blowing her nose. "His behavior wears me down. He wants to control me. This is what happens all the time. He's angry. I'm upset. He criticizes me and then won't talk to me. Then I get angry and say things I shouldn't, and Doug retaliates. We go around and around. I just don't think I can take it anymore. I want out."

"I do *not* want a divorce," said Doug. "I love Jackie, and I want the marriage." When he said that, Jackie instantly switched her position and said she loved him too but did not want to be upset constantly.

Critical Labels

Critical communication follows a pattern. A pattern of critical words eventually establishes labels that develop a grid in the mind. Critical labels include the following: slow, dumb, mean, selfish, poor house-keeper, poor provider, and more.

Doug labeled Jackie as scatterbrained, impulsive, and angry. Jackie labeled Doug as critical, mean, and controlling. Their habitual thoughts easily reinforced the labels. Doug's criticisms are "she jumps from one thing to another and can't even keep the house clean" and Jackie's criticisms are "he views me as stupid and incompetent—how mean" accelerated their negative feelings about one another.

People establish labels in their minds to enable themselves to think faster. Labels set up grids in which words and behavior dock without thought. For example, Doug might say, "She has a lot on her mind," meaning she was forgetful with good reason, but if he called her scatterbrained instead, indicating she was incapable of thinking straight, the label would define her mind as deficient and would automatically drop into Doug's silent preset grid as *stupid*, even though he had verbalized that she was not stupid.

The grid is sticky. Labels are not easily shaken, and each negative thought reinforces the relevant label while the thought drives the relationship deeper into dislike and distrust.

Individual Sessions

The next sessions were separate meetings with Jackie and Doug; people are different when alone. Often, individuals provide important or secret information that can alter the counseling path. For example, revealing a partner's violent temper during a session or disclosing an affair that is in process or over may be overwhelming to the unsuspecting partner. Shocked or embarrassed, the person may leap up and shoot out of the room, never to be seen in my office again. (This has happened!)

In this case, a private talk with Jackie was necessary because I suspected she might have ADD (attention deficit disorder), given her difficulty concentrating. When I asked if she had ever considered this possibility, she said, "I did have difficulty in school; I couldn't sit still. Testing was suggested, but my parents refused; in fact, they were insulted, so the idea was dropped. Do you think I have ADD?"

"I think it would be a good idea to check it out."

"I would be relieved, because despite what Doug says, I do feel stupid a lot. Like a kid, I go from one thing to another without finishing anything."

Jackie discovered she had ADD and was given medication, which she found helpful, but it did not solve their habitual negative interactions.

Goal Setting

There are couples that need to bicker, argue, and destroy good feelings. They may be masochists, they may be control freaks, they may be obsessive, and they may repress the disturbance and consequently have no motivation to change. However, Jackie and Doug stated vehemently that they hated their communication style, yet their critical tit-for-tat behavior had continued unabated for twelve years.

Their stated goal in marriage counseling was to dramatically alter their damaging interactions and live together peacefully.

"You both agree that critical communication is a major problem?" I asked.

They both answered yes.

"Let's immediately begin by altering the way you talk to each other. By that, I mean burrow down to your communication cores, and give yourselves relief from daily critical, angry, and verbal battering. I want you to work on repeating the following concepts to yourselves. The following items may sound like baby steps—they are."

I gave them the following list of ideas that they needed to memorize:

- I am responsible for my words.
- I acknowledge that I have been critical and I am sorry.
- I will not speak critically. I will muffle any critical words that come to mind.
- I need help. If you (spouse) hear critical words, please tell me.
- Tell me verbally or in writing.
- I am happy to have you help me. I want you to help me.

"To point out critical words to each other may seem like throwing a hand grenade without expecting an explosion, but to share a common goal means you are a team, so work together without rancor. Your job is to shut off the negative motor mind, listen carefully while the other person is talking, and then acknowledge your partner's words and emotions without negative interpretations.

"If the inner critic won't be stifled, either stop talking or step into another room—be quiet and rethink the situation. The method is not perfect, but when it does work and you talk together, the connection will be reinforced; in turn, you will feel that your marriage still has possibilities and potential.

Wrap Up

Jackie and Doug began their marriage counseling ready for battle, and each either jumped into agitated talk or tiptoed around, waiting for the other person's first angry volley. However, their paying attention to their own thoughts and words before speaking calmed them and gradually eliminated the snappy, critical attacks, the nasty reactions, and the necessity to defend fractured egos.

Because Jackie and Doug were dedicated and actively sought positive action, they were able to change their brain grids from fearing personal attacks to seeking a peaceful coexistence. These are the three things that finally altered Jackie's attitude: ADD testing, understanding her own issues, and finding calm within herself.

Eight months of counseling ended with peace and lighthearted laughter—a striking change from the day they set foot in my office.

CHAPTER 19
Criticism and Complaints

Jackie and Doug worked together to alter their relationship and eliminate critical comments. You, on the other hand, may have decided that marriage counseling is necessary to put an end to incessant critical talk, but perhaps your spouse is dead set against seeking any help. In that case, dedication to your own transformation will alter your partnership—you can change your life dramatically all by yourself.

You might be thinking, "What about my partner? My partner should stop criticizing and upsetting me."

Yes, your partner should. We will figure out how to handle this critical style later, but are you going to wait for your partner's change, or will you take command of yourself? To realistically examine your own behavior is the first step.

First, clear your slate. Examine your interactions. Is there any possibility that you are overly critical, either by your own or by your partner's assessment? Do you do any of the following?

- Criticize
- Complain
- Become irritated easily

- Overreact or attack
- Jump to conclusions
- Exaggerate or minimize
- Act depressed and moody
- Act defensive if there is an indication your partner is displeased
- Educate

The last item needs particular attention. When you are the educator in a relationship, you assume that you know best and then definitively communicate your knowledge, or you believe that your communication style may be helpful. In regard to the concept of education, quickly jot down a yes or no to the following items. Are you

- A good listener?
- Patient?
- Loving?
- Solution oriented?
- Insight oriented?
- Accommodating?
- Kind and generous?

"Be honest," I said to Jackie. "Is there anything in the above sixteen statements that you need to change?

"In addition, keep track of thoughts in response to your partner's words for a week; if you do, you will discover a very interesting life form. Your brain has patterned communication maps, which often turn out to be critical habits of thought. For example, your husband may ask, 'Would you come out and snip the top of the bushes while I mow?' In response, you say yes, but your mind thinks, 'Damn it! For crying out loud, you big baby, I'm working in the house, but now I have to help you too. Don't you think I have better things to do than follow you around?'

"You do not address issues. You mumble to yourself and get angry with your husband. Critical thinking is increasing tension in your marriage, and since your husband is not a mind reader, tension cannot be resolved without a discussion.

"When you have concrete information about your habitual pattern of acting and reacting, instead of responding with blurry, defensive comments— 'I didn't mean that' or 'I didn't say that' or 'I am right'—know that you have ammunition for yourself and need to work on specific thoughts and behavior. Defensive comments are not needed.

"Congratulate yourself for positive behaviors, and then choose a critical behavior you want to alter or eliminate. Methods to regularly remind yourself are critical since good ideas and plans to change vaporize easily. Here is a suggestion: write your plan in code on your cell phone and any other private place. It is important that you are not nagged about change. Don't let anyone say things like, 'Oh, so you are going to change—right!' Before you make any announcement about your personal dedication to altering your behavior, make sure others will be helpful; otherwise, sabotage will soon follow your announcement."

Altering Your Response in the Face Of Criticism

It is difficult to handle a critical partner and remain emotionally unfazed. The tendency is either to absorb the insults quietly or to argue fruitlessly. To stop the habit of folding when you are criticized and to learn to stand up for yourself and effectively argue both sound easy, but if you have put up with criticism, it may be difficult to talk to your partner with ease. Your reaction has probably been pitifully defensive or ineffectively aggressive.

Mentally practice what you will say in the face of critical words. Practice simple phrases until they are second nature, and then speak directly the moment you hear a critical remark. For example, "I realize you may not mean to criticize me" or "you may not be aware that those words are critical, but they hurt my feelings."

If your partner responds with something like "so what?" or "you are too sensitive" or "you are misinterpreting my words," stand your ground. Do not cave. Do not argue. Your partner is dodging, being defensive, or being downright aggressive. Stay clear headed, even though your heart might be pounding and you feel nervous. This person is a bully. You are stating a fact, and if your words are thrown back at you, the discussion is over.

While your memory is clear, immediately go to your computer or journal and jot down exactly what has been said. Fear, anticipatory anxiety, or argumentative defensiveness is keeping you spinning and stuck in an emotional quagmire. A transcript will reveal facts.

The point is to shine a spotlight on reality so that you can calm down, think clearly, react only to facts, and establish a plan of conscious, effective word action.

Conscious Words and Acts

Once words are spoken, they cannot be taken back. You can think anything and dismiss thoughts, but spoken words penetrate other people's minds and may never leave. Mean-spirited words, criticism, and constant complaining—as well as the negative experience of disrespect, contempt, and silence—are chilling intimacy breakers.

Criticism is different than contempt. Contempt, explored in the next chapter, distorts character and globally undermines a person's personality. But first, let's look at the annoying whiner.

Alicia: The Whiner

Even therapists get tired of a critical complainer. It is one thing to verbalize unhappiness and look for a solution, but Alicia, a thirty-eight-year-old, had spent her life angry and whining about past and present misery, and she continued to complain in therapy.

Alicia presented herself as unable to change any thought process. In her first therapy session, she said, "Why am I always unhappy? I love my house, but I don't want to do anything in my house. I'm always negative with Hank, my live-in friend. Then he gets mad. I don't want to touch him or really have anything to do with him, even though Hank does everything for me. He cleans the house and makes dinner. He's generous, but I'm just not happy."

I asked Alicia when she started to feel that way.

"I'm not sure. I think since we bought the house. I know when we were going together I thought Hank was nice looking and nice to me. We hardly ever had sex then because he had a problem, but he has had a penile implant since then. He really just did it for me.

"Even so, I don't want to have sex with him. Isn't that awful? I went with Tony for four years, and we had sex all the time. I couldn't wait to get my hands on him, but with Hank, I'm not interested. I say mean things to him too. I don't know why."

A Dedicated Complainer

Alicia was a complainer who declared that everything and everybody had been thrust upon her. She had been feeling unhappy and complaining for years. Her relationship with Hank was the first one she had with a nice man, she said. All the other men in her life had run around with other women or were married—except her first husband, who she fought with all the time. "He was mean and verbally abusive. Still, I wish I hadn't divorced my first husband. I keep thinking that, and I even tell Hank that. Then I wouldn't have to work.

"I'm mad at him because I shouldn't have to work, and he gets angry with me for no good reason."

The present was not reality. Alicia was living in her past misery and clinging to her unhappiness as if it were a badge of honor. She had no choice but to wallow in pity. She repeatedly asks me, "Why do I do that?" Meaning that she wanted to know why she kept thinking such thoughts.

I asked, "Yes, that's a good question. Why do you continuously think those thoughts?"

Alicia smirked, and I know we were doing a 180-degree turn back to where we started.

Alicia, like a ping-pong ball, called for therapy every couple of years, which told me she was interested either in change or in complaining to someone besides Hank, but in those two years, she never matured enough to grasp that she was responsible for her thoughts and, therefore, her life.

Complaint as a Lifestyle

Alicia harped, scolded, and complained continuously. She had a defensive complaint style that kept others away while she pleasantly wallowed in her unhappiness.

If you live with a person like Alicia you need bold, businesslike survival techniques. Here is a list of things you can do and keep in mind:

1. Write down the words of the complaint exactly.
2. Ask yourself if the words have validity.
3. Reacting with anger, sullen behavior, or withdrawal is not effective.
4. Neutralize your thoughts about the complaints before you discuss specific words. You want to be objective and learn what is going on in your partner's mind (maybe nothing is).
5. Tell your partner you want to sit down at a convenient time and talk. Decide when and where together, but do not let the matter drop. If a time is not suggested, you set the time.

6. When you discuss complaints, begin by reading exact words. Do not editorialize.

7. Do not allow any diversionary subjects to take you away from the point you were making.

8. Your job is to find out what your spouse is thinking. You need information.

9. If the words reflect a problem with your behavior or your words, take them seriously and examine yourself.

10. If the words are simply mean spirited and meant to hurt, the next time a complaint is aimed at you, try to understand the mind they came from. Do not jump for the bait and get pulled into the complaint vortex.

Whatever the outcome, you are putting your partner on notice that you will no longer simply react; instead, you will have a calm discussion. And with this information, you gain the opportunity to alter your interactions; thus, you will either make changes or accept that you will be chained to an unhappy, dissatisfied person forever.

The next chapters focus on how to handle the issues of contempt, sarcasm, and the refusal to speak.

CHAPTER 20
Contempt

John M. Gottman, PhD, is a psychologist who has spent twenty years studying married couples to determine which personality traits result in relationship satisfaction and which lead to relationship failure. Dr. Gottman found that when partners are treated with contempt, sooner or later their partnerships end. Relationships cannot withstand contempt; *contempt* means "treating a partner without consideration, as worthless or despicable."

Sharon and Brad

Sharon and Brad called for marriage counseling when they finally acknowledged that talking together and being happy were an oxymoron. *Confusion* was the operative word to describe their relationship; to decode their verbal and physical messages was a complex undertaking. Contemptuous words had a way of creeping into every conversation.

A simple conversation between Sharon and Brad was an emotionally disturbing experience, in which the intent of communication—that is, to connect—was lost. Instead, their words were used to baffle, express disdain, or a call for combat. Their relationship comprised blatant contempt that lead to physical abuse.

Sharon and Brad lived together on an emotional edge. They could not wait for a chance to express contemptuous words couched in innocent-sounding bewilderment. For example, Sharon asked Brad, "What are you talking about?" Brad said, "For God's sake, Sharon, are you brain dead, pretending you don't get it, or just trying to make me mad?"

Who was the culprit in that exchange? Was Sharon baiting Brad, as he implied, or was he taking an opportunity to criticize and express hostility?

They were perpetually volatile, ready to explode at a moment's notice. Their feelings simmered as they waited for the right look, the right twitch, or the right word to give them license to fight. A mix of subtle or in-your-face contempt fed their waiting. Both were always eager to utter their "I gotcha!" refrain.

Marriage Counseling

Sharon and Brad walked into their first marriage-counseling session holding hands. They sat down and declared their undying love for each other and agreed that their most-troubling problems were their daily arguments and fights with occasional physical bouts.

"When you say 'physical bouts,' what exactly are you talking about?"

Sharon said, "Brad is critical and has a temper, but he can contain it with loud talk or by yelling. I seem to need to poke him or hit him—not hard—when I'm upset. Then he grabs me, and that's about it."

Brad was staring at Sharon. He leaned forward and said, "Sweetheart, tell the truth."

"Well, sometimes I feel as if I have to whack him to get his attention."

"Have either of you ever had to call 911?"

Sharon jumped in. "Brad called once. We were calm when the police came, so they left, but they did warn us that spousal abuse results in jail time. The law takes it seriously, and we were told to see a counselor. That was a few years ago."

"And did you see a counselor?"

They said no at the same time; then they smiled.

"I notice that both of you are smiling. What's that about?"

Sharon hesitated. "I think we feel silly and embarrassed."

I said, "I also take the use of physical force seriously. From this moment forward, we need to agree that talk is your method of communication; marriage counseling is a forum for conversation, expressing feelings verbally, and solving problems. A tap or a slap—anything physical—is not playful and is not acceptable, ever!

"Can we make a pact that you will not touch one another in anger or in any disrespectful manner while you are in marriage counseling?"

They agreed, and in the next session, I had a written agreement for each to sign.

Unlike the angry, ready-to-fight person described earlier, in therapy Brad, thirty-three, was soft spoken and personable, and he had very definite ideas about everything, from child rearing to what should be on National Public Radio. Fit and tan, he was an ex-hockey coach turned sales rep for wholesale wines. He had happily taken on the role of dad for Sharon's three children, ages four to sixteen. Sharon was enamored with Brad's child-rearing and husband orientation--dad as head of the household and boss was like honey to a bee.

Sharon loved the idea of Brad as the family's protector. She just could not agree with his family-man style. Sharon, thirty-seven, was Brad's counterpart. Where he smiled, fit in, and quietly moved around, Sharon was an in-your-face live wire, whose unusual appearance matched her personality. Her features and coloring did not quite fit together: her unusually large mouth and teeth skewed her blue eyes, light hair, and olive skin. Sharon's mouth fit her personality: she was boisterous and argumentative.

Sitting together on the couch in my office, Sharon gazed into Brad's eyes, paused, and then quietly posed a question to me. She wanted to know who was right. "I have an example for you. On Saturday mornings, I go to college. Brad goes to work at 11:00 a.m., but he takes care of my four-year-old, Melanie, until her father, Joe, appears to pick her up.

"Last Saturday, Brad told me he called Joe at 11:10 a.m. Joe hadn't shown up, and Brad was agitated and, I suppose, worried about getting to work. Joe had told him to 'f—— off' and that he'd get there when he was good and ready. Brad exploded, and Joe hung up on him.

"I got home from school a few minutes later, and I totally agreed with Brad. I called Joe and began to chew him out, but Brad told me to calm down. 'Not in front of Mel,' he said. I agreed.

"Brad left for work, and I thought everything was cool. Then came the bomb, and this is what always happens. Brad called from his cell phone and began to talk quietly about Joe's behavior. He said he was shocked that I hadn't stood up for him. He was disgusted with me. If the situation had been reversed, he would not have put up with it.

"We are constantly in a state where I think we are on the same track and doing what Brad wants when—wham—he slams me." Sharon's shrill tone was escalating.

Brad was not going to take that lying down. He said, "My whole damn job on the weekends is to keep Sharon calm—Saturday was no exception. When I left that morning, I could tell she was seething, so I called her from my car just to make sure she was okay." He trailed off as if he was so disgusted with her rendition of reality, implying that it was useless to even talk.

Word Power

In general, Brad laid the groundwork for trouble by quietly making provocative statements. He said, "By the way, I noticed that the kids are falling behind in their chores, probably because they aren't being supervised like we agreed."

Sharon sat up straight and stared at Brad. "What?" she said, nearly shouting.

Gazing at her with what appeared to be love and tenderness, Brad said, "I'm sorry you are so thin skinned." Then he began to defend and explain himself, pointing out that she was wrong and that his feelings were hurt by her words. Because of his calm, quiet, and definitive presentation, Sharon could not figure out how to express herself. She flew at his words and then became the goat, hysterical and aggressive, the person who started the fight.

Whose interpretation of reality was the real truth? How did Sharon and Brad come to vie for the status of the victim, the person who was slighted and misunderstood?

History

Sharon teared up and had trouble sharing stories about her history. After a few false starts, she began with the disappearance of her mother when she was four. She was left with her father, who others considered a charming drunk, and three siblings—a six-month-old, a one-year-old, and a three-year-old. Her father ignored the children, particularly the baby. Sharon took on the mother role, and she was criticized and punished as though she were an adult.

Sharon's home was located in a poor town in Michigan's upper peninsula. Neighbors helped care for the children as best they could, sharing milk and boxes of cereal, asking the children in for peanut butter and jelly sandwiches and warmth. CPS (child protective services) was occasionally notified when one or more of the children were outside, unsupervised, dirty, dressed inappropriately, or undressed. They often went without shoes and at times were locked out.

When CPS visited, Sharon's father would become furious, which caused more trouble for the children, but according to Sharon, they were rescued from being sent to foster care because their grandmother made occasional visits, which appeased CPS.

Brad, on the other hand, lived in a military family with strict rules and regulations. His father expected full cooperation from Brad and his brother—or else. The boys had difficulty complying because they never fully understood which instruction was in operation at what time. Punishment was a leather-strap whipping.

The brothers angrily talked to each other about their father's brutality and what they would do to their father when they were old enough. Unfortunately, Brad's father died when Brad was fourteen, a turbulent age made more difficult by the loss of a loved and hated parent.

After his father's death, guilt and shame were Brad's coping mechanism, methods he continued to use as an adult. In his relationship with Sharon, he would shame her and then indirectly apologize.

Neither Sharon's nor Brad's childhood provided a loving home life with the guidance and understanding needed by a growing child. Both had felt criticized and misunderstood; each had felt abandoned, alone, and unprotected. Contemptuous words sliced at the core of their beings, coloring and distorting what they heard. In their relationship, they clung to each other like abused children, but at the same time, they lashed out critically. However, respites of "love" that reforged their loosely knit bond were interspersed among their frequent lashings.

In marriage and life, our jobs are to grow and develop, which requires that we mature and learn from experience. Instead of maturing, Sharon and Brad were boxed in together and frightened each other. They acted out their deepest, most primitive fear by casting fear's shadow on each other. Without really listening and understanding Brad's words, Sharon would feel attacked and would react immediately and abrasively.

Whenever Sharon spoke, Brad felt rejected, angry, and perplexed, as he did as a child, and would respond with sly character assassinations. They experienced perverse pleasure in dramatically expressing angry criticism and contemptuous words, and then they would become huffy, agitated, or furious about the other person's mirroring behavior.

Therapy

Sharon and Brad's style of talking represented their convoluted childhood feelings. Their talk would wander into misunderstandings and feelings of being personally attacked. Their contemptuous words were meant to put each other down, squash each other's ego, and elevate the talker. There was no insightful, rational communication.

Communication, the ability to talk and listen, is necessary to grasp another person's feelings, to clarify thoughts, and to make sense of the here and now, but the underlying communication style of Sharon and Brad was a more fundamental problem. They had self-esteem issues, which began in childhood, when they learned to protect their fragile child egos with childish defenses—defenses that became ineffective in their adult lives but kept them rooted in thinking and responding immaturely. Each of them had replaced the other's feared parent.

There is a fork in the developmental road where children may become conscious that their models, parents, siblings, friends, cultures, or environments are not in their best interest. If children experience adult behavior that is frightening, bewildering, or irrational, they cannot make sense of it. An example of this type of adult would be a religious male parent who is an alcoholic. He often attacks his wife and is mean spirited and nasty to the children when drunk, but in church, he presents himself as a loving and caring husband and father.

Children's conscious reconfiguration of their parents' contradictory behaviors will depersonalize and attribute the lack of attention and love and mean or cruel behavior to where the behavior belongs—to their parents. The first focus of therapy is to stop the word battles, to calm and untangle communication experiences, and to set up boundaries. Boundaries establish a realm in which a person is allowed to express his or her feelings honestly, and the other person is allowed to disagree.

Listening is an art, and it requires a quiet, conscious mind. Partners need to follow these key principles when they are trying to communicate and listen:

- Stop before you utter a negative word or phrase—even midsentence.
- If your partner tells you that your words are negative or hurtful, at that moment acknowledge that that is what your partner thinks and feels. You are not responsible for his or her thoughts and feelings.
- Do not dispute or argue! Expect your mind to throw up arguments and defensive thoughts. Do not verbalize those thoughts.
- When your partner speaks, do not immediately respond. Take a few seconds to sooth and calm yourself. Preface any communication with "I understand that you think..." After doing so, present your version of what you have just heard in a soft voice. If you are confused, say so. Stay calm and listen until you understand.
- If you cannot remain calm, you are the problem, not your partner.

Quieting the mind was a difficult task for these two, but they worked at it as if they were in school and about to be tested. Rectifying their communication patterns proceeded unevenly, as expected, but they persisted for two years. The beauty of quieting the mind allowed them to hear their self-talk, creating a juncture at which mindfulness began.

Long-Term Solution

Both individual and joint therapy sessions were necessary to stop the verbal bloodletting between those two. Individual psychotherapy, along with marriage counseling, probed and exposed their skewed personal perspectives, which had kept them cocooned with damaged images and feelings. Psychotherapy was an opportunity to delve into who they were in the present and what they could expect; psychotherapy also provided learning tools that enabled them to appreciate and work with—not against—each other.

To understand that feelings are often historically rooted in learned behavior is freeing. For example, when Brad would look at Sharon quizzically, she would register that look as critical anger—her father's look. That look might actually reflect that emotion, or it might be that Brad simply did not understand whatever she had just said.

However, whenever she responded sharply, he would become defensive and strike back, and around they would go. Those feelings were habitual, ground-in responses. Consequently, they needed time and months of patience to learn to stop, step back, and recognize their unhealthy and automatic responses before responding.

Sharon and Brad surprised me with their steady, tenacious therapy work; they attended every appointment and eventually dropped their critical views and harmful words directed toward each other. I was happy to tell them how proud I was of their ability to change their brains (a very difficult task!), to let go of angry, contemptuous words, and to allow love to be their focus.

CHAPTER 21
Sarcasm

Sarcasm is an accelerated and virulent form of criticism. Where criticism finds faults and makes judgments, sarcasm is filled with mocking, acerbic remarks. Though witty at times, sarcastic comments make use of biting, indirect words to slide into a person's mind and rip apart inner peace. These words are accompanied by subtle facial nuances that indicate the recipient is discounted and probably dumb.

Though you know you have been maligned and immediately *feel* the message, interpretation may take a minute to register. If you protest and indicate you are upset by the implication, tone, or words, you will be met by responses that may imply any of the following opinions:

- You are too sensitive.
- You lack understanding.
- You take everything too seriously.
- You lack a sense of humor.
- You made your partner mad by your response.
- You don't know how to communicate.
- You deserve what was just said.

People who resort to sarcasm are word bullies who are uninterested in your protestations; rather, they feel justified by their sarcastic style and view themselves as clever and in command.

Sarcasm with children is an abuse of power; sarcasm with adults is a form of verbal abuse. The intent of sarcasm is to raise yourself in your own eyes and diminish the other person. It is meant to harm and injure the other person's character.

Both private and public arenas are venues for sarcasm. In public, sarcasm has qualities of humiliation and embarrassment, and if those present are silent, the sarcastic individual takes silence as tacit approval and confirmation of the abuse. Family members may not speak up to protect their loved ones to avoid an altercation; people may laugh, but sarcasm usually leaves any audience uneasy. In private, sarcasm can be constant and dedicated. The person who is attacked may seem only dimly aware and even deny the abuse.

The result of growing up with a generation of mean parents follows.

Judith

Judith was a solid, big-boned woman. She wore little makeup and styled her hair in a simple manner, though she had enough curls to indicate that she had a perm somewhere along the way. She wore expensive tailored clothes and completed her ensemble with scuffed shoes. She had been married and divorced several times.

In her first therapy session, Judith stated that her family was her problem. "If I call my kids, who are grown, they talk to me for about two minutes max, seldom accept invitations to visit, and—this really hurts me—none of them invite me over."

Judith said her children told her they do not appreciate the way she talks to them. "I'm occasionally sarcastic. I'm being funny, and they know I'm just joking."

"Do they laugh?"

"They don't seem to have a sense of humor."

"If your kids aren't laughing, then they don't know you are joking. Your understanding is that if they take your words seriously, they are in error."

Judith was insulted by my comment and said so.

I explained that sarcasm is a defense usually learned in childhood and that it claims innocence while refusing responsibility for hurting other people's feelings. Judith nodded. Nodding was her way to acknowledge that what I was saying might have something to do with her behavior; at the same time, she stared at the wall behind me, expressionless.

The Disconnect

Judith, forty-three, knew who she was in the business world. She was powerful, third in command in a large insurance company. She said that in her workplace, she could make decisions and solve any problems with a sense of humor.

Her idea of humor, however, was sometimes interpreted differently by others.

Others' sarcastic comments destroyed her, while she viewed her sarcasm as funny and lighthearted. When her family responded to her comments by disappearing or replying sarcastically, Judith would feel indignant and offended. For example, when her daughter was struggling to remember an incident that had occurred years ago, Judith called her a bobblehead and then laughed. She could not believe her daughter was upset by her comment.

Mean Parents Beget Mean Parents

Sarcasm that sounds confident, bold, and aggressive is based on fear. Judith learned in her original family to be exquisitely sensitive to her own emotions and, at the same time, to ignore the feelings of others.

She was devastated by hurtful comments, just as she was when her critical, authoritarian mother would screech and rage and say, "Get out of my sight. You make me sick—what's wrong with you?" Also, her mother would continually say, "I'm sorry I ever had a child like you."

"Can you remember how you felt about your mother's comments?" I asked.

"I feel a little upset right now discussing the past, but I can't remember feeling anything."

When she was in seventh grade, she was honored for her artistic ability at a school banquet. Her mother told her after she accepted the award, "couldn't you have thought of something better to say?" Her mother then said that Judith had walked up to accept the award like a cripple.

These and many other contemptuous parental words and behaviors swirled together and baked Judith's feelings and taught the relationship portion of her thought processes to be on guard and ready to attack. However, she learned not to be as in-your-face mean as her mother was; instead, she learned to use clever but underhanded sarcasm that was hurtful.

With good reason, Judith failed in her development to launch past the need to protect her ego. As an adult, Judith no longer needed to protect herself and ward off the blows and arrows of childhood, but the habit of sarcasm lived on, invisible to her.

Immediate Problem

The first issue was to recognize and acknowledge her habitual sarcasm. The second was to spell out specifics: when, where, and with whom was she sarcastic.

"Do you recognize your sarcastic comments?"

"Not really. I think I've blocked them. I'm occasionally sarcastic but appropriate; I do not want to walk in my mother's footsteps."

"'Appropriate' is your defense. You are here because your adult children are upset by your sarcastic treatment of them. Your stance is that they should not be distressed. In other words, you should be able to say and do whatever you want, and they better like it. But they don't. Your sarcastic words are not appropriate. If you are interested in improving relationships, as you say, it's time to delve into and solve the problem. Is that correct?"

In a formal tone, she said, "You're the expert," with an emphasis on the word *expert*.

I waited several seconds and said, "I'll take that as a yes, you agree, but I did note that your sarcasm is alive and well."

Judith's lips curled up slightly.

"Did you realize you were using sarcasm when you said, 'You're the expert'?"

"After I said it and saw your face, I realized it was a zinger. I'm sorry."

"You may not realize it, but you smiled slightly so that I immediately questioned 'sorry'. You don't need words to relay contempt—body language tells the whole story. Facial disgust, sneering, curling lips, or rolling eyes indicate contempt and display people's thoughts.

"The fact that you are aware of your tendency to be sarcastic and are actively seeking to kick the habit is exceptional. This behavior has not been your friend, but in my opinion, you have the perfect personality to conquer and replace your sarcastic thoughts with a positive mind-set.

"Now, let's decide exactly how to attack your habit."

Judith Begins the Solution Process

"Sarcasm is mean spirited and has negative consequences, but since sarcastic thoughts naturally come to your mind, as we just saw, eliminating the sarcastic slice and dice mode will be difficult. Be prepared for resistance from yourself because there is powerful pleasure in the sarcastic sucker-punch feeling of control.

"Also, be prepared to be tenacious. Enter into a contract with yourself just as you would with your employees. Managing sarcasm requires an unnatural amount of self-attention to and separation from your defensive ego, which feels pleasure when you put down and control other people and situations, as well as the real, loving, and connected you.

"When you are told your words hurt, whether you believe they do or do not hurt, accept that others have a right to their experience. Just tell them you're sorry. The minute you realize you have spoken sarcastically, apologize. Whether the realization comes seconds after you have spoken or two days later, acknowledge to yourself and to that person that you were inappropriate.

"Catalog situations, particular people, and how or why you react sarcastically. Visual written proof provides facts that cannot be swept away.

"Rehearse positive responses. Thoughts that come to mind do not need to be spoken. Plan ahead to divert yourself if your mind feels out of control.

"Stay conscious. The minute you resort to old unconscious habits, your old words will surface.

"As an executive, you order others to make alterations. Order your own alterations and stick with them."

The Brave Family Solution

"So far, you have been talking to yourself. The following action—to open yourself up to the family as part of the sarcasm solution—will be more difficult. You will put yourself in a vulnerable position and need to be prepared.

"Tell your family that you are working on changing and need their help to recognize your sarcastic words and behavior. Keep in mind that you are handing them a hammer and that if they wish to use it, their responses may hurt your feelings. Tell them you want to eliminate barriers, to love each and every one of them, and to be closer emotionally.

"Your family is a learning machine. You are a model, whether good or bad. In your case, by easing sarcasm out of your life, your children will be proud and respect your desire to eliminate relationship barriers. They are old enough to understand how difficult it is to expose a vulnerable part of one's self.

"It is important to prepare yourself, to gear up, and to think about how others may respond and how you will depersonalize. For example, someone may say something like "Judith, why would you want to change? I've always enjoyed your witticism," but you must remember that such thoughts belong to other people and that other people's ideas have nothing to do with you. Let them say whatever. If their words are not in your best interest, so what? They are simply telling you who they are.

"You have a detailed job to do: First, inform your family members of your plan. Tell them you are aware of your hurtful sarcasm and are actively working on eradicating it. Second, remember that your family can be helpful to you by pointing out sarcastic comments but only if you prepare yourself for their comments and are graceful in receiving those comments. Third, the minute you feel hurt or angry, settle down, take a deep breath, and remember your goal. Fourth, remember that because this is a long-term project, patience is required. Fifth, remember that you are not trying to change anyone else, so skip educational talk."

In therapy, Judith's sarcastic style received a psychological chelation. Chelation exchanges sick bodily fluids for healthy blood; Judith was exchanging poisonous old thoughts for healthy new ideas and understanding. Just like a marrow transplant, the diseased experience is examined, extricated, and replaced.

Talking about change is simple; putting new ideas into effect can be hard. Currently, Judith is still attending therapy, continuously working with herself, making a sustained effort to control her words, and trying to overcome hurt feelings as she turns herself into a loving person and receives intentional and unintentional payback. Judith's family is warming up to her, but they have not exactly welcomed her with open arms. They have been hurt in the past, so it will take time for them to trust her recovery from her sarcastic mind-set.

Just as the noise of inner or outer words is a form of communication, so is the deafening sound of silence.

CHAPTER 22
Silence

Deliberate silence is a form of communication called *withholding*. Without words, you can only guess what your partner is thinking, often an educated guess, but unless your partner reveals his or her thoughts, you will be left in the dark. If people feel so strongly that speaking is not possible after the occurrence of relationship disturbances, their taking time to think about and then talk about the issues is a positive conclusion. If, instead, your partner maintains an icy distance, you can assume that you are being controlled by silence.

A partner who goes for days without talking is stonewalling. Realistically and intellectually, you might view this behavior as childish, but isn't it weird that silence can put you into a tense, anxious, or angry state? Even though you know that your partner will not speak about their anger when the issue is over, still you experience tension and live in your mind with the knowledge that the problem cannot be talked out. As a result, you carry on without a solution and pretend everything is alright.

Before you take the high ground and point out how silence stands in the way of understanding relationship problems, examine your own communication. Are you part of the problem? Do you overtalk? Do you allow your partner free expression without interrupting? Do you insist so vehemently on your version of reality that negotiation becomes impossible? Do you put down any ideas other than your own?

Be honest, and if any of those scenarios are true, mention the communication style and the difficulties you have in expressing yourself, when the conversation resumes. If you are seriously altering your communication habits, point out that fact as well. If you have not found any fault with yourself, you might check your style of communication with your partner. If she or he indicates there is an issue, do not deny it, do not explain it away, and do not let your partner know that he or she is just plain wrong. It is critical to understand that your partner chooses silence as a method to control the situation and that you are playing a role.

Are you beginning to disengage? Are you ready to dig deeper into your reactions?

If the relationship is important, the following suggestions will help resolve your emotional reactions to your partner's silence with anxiety, depression, anger, or fear—all of which may rumble through your mind while you wait hours or days until the wall of silence slips away:

- Direct your mind to calm down, and stay calm.
- Stop dwelling on the silence. Acknowledge and release focus.
- Devise a silence plan.
- You do not have to communicate. You feel uncomfortable with the silence, but so what?
- Go about your business. Silence is an opportunity to think your own thoughts.

Resolution will come through your mind-set. You are probably living with a scared, silent person who is immobilized. It is important for you to stay off the train of fear. You need not be immobilized as well. Talk to yourself, and write down positives and negatives about the issues, the situations, and your partner's behavior.

Here is an example list of positives and negatives:

Positives
We do not fight.
I like having alone time.
I do not need to know why my partner is angry with me.
I prefer silence to anger.

Negatives
We do not talk.
I feel lonely.
Emotions are not expressed.
I cannot stand silence.

By writing a list of positives and negatives, you will qualify the here and now and will stay away from running around like a rat in a maze of questions with no answers. Let the need to shut you out remain your partner's issue, not yours.

Knowledge is power. Once you firmly grasp the fact that silence is your partner's communication style, you put yourself in charge. At that point, you become able to work with your partner, to put up with your silent partner, or to consider other possibilities.

PART FOUR

Thought Disorders: Domino, Distortion, Dissociation, And Personalization

Part 4 describes four thinking disorders: domino, distortion, dissociation, and personalization—all of which result in communication chaos. Where silence is obvious control and shuts communication down, thinking disorders disturb and confuse relationships.

Some people's brains are wired with talk that disrupts, distracts, and circles back, producing a frustrating, constant need for clarification. If you live with a person whose thinking is disordered and if you do not have a transcript to untangle ordinary conversation that swivels into troubled talk, clarification is next to impossible. A cognitively disordered person does not recognize his or her issue but is definite about who is causing the difficulty—You!

The result of this struggle is confusion that causes fights about what has been said. You will feel defensive and distrust your own perceptions. These experiences are a fissure that cracks partners' rapport and prevents them from connecting.

Clarification

Once you recognize there is a difference between conversation that connects and troubled talk and see that your relationship is embroiled in rambling conversations that lead nowhere, you turn the corner toward a solution.

The following information will help you make sense out of what seems to be and often is nonsense. The information will assist your recognition of emotions generated by cloudy words and go-nowhere sentences.

CHAPTER 23

Domino

Domino talk is a form of circular talk: some information is involved, but you do not know what to make of it. A simple question begins a long response that meanders with irrelevant details but has no apparent end point.

For example, you ask your wife a simple question: "Where were you?"

Instead of giving a straight answer, she says, "Why do you question me all the time?" Then she begins the dissertation. "Well, Joan called about three o'clock and said she was going to Saks and wanted me to go along, but I told her I had too much to do, so…" She continues without coming to a conclusion.

You feel frustrated and agitated by the long response. You show impatience and dissatisfaction, so she gets upset and accusatory because you asked a question but then did not listen to the answer.

Negative emotions flare up. The result? Once miscommunication takes hold, you fall into communication quicksand, sucked into a bewildering chaos, where talking only compounds the problem.

Although you feel that change is critical, you may find whining and complaining to yourself is easier than taking action, thereby setting yourself up as a helpless victim. "What can I do about the way she thinks and talks? Nothing," you say to yourself. By accepting her communication style, you are doing the domino dance with her.

Many paragraphs into her reply, you lose interest but remain a participant, indicating to her that she has captured your attention. Or you let her know you are angry and sick of listening. "That's it!" you say. "Never mind! Getting an answer from you is impossible."

She says, "What's wrong with you? You never listen. You aren't interested in me or anything I do."

And a nasty argument ensues.

The Lone Solution
Wait until you and your partner are calm, whether cooling off takes hours or days. Let your partner know you are eager to solve communication issues. You must remain calm when your partner says things like, "What are you talking about? You have the problem—you don't listen. If you would just listen to me, we would be fine. You need therapy."

Now you know you are on your own, but you do have a choice: continue the solution process for your own edification or accept the confusion you live in.

Exactly why are these conversations troubling? Think of yourself as a scientist and miscommunication as a fact. It is important to know what you are responding to and what words, looks, or tones disturb you.

When you examine your negative encounters, transcribe the words as closely as possible. Describe and write your exact feelings. For example, imagine an encounter in which your partner says, "Why are you always questioning me?" What is more, he or she does not wait for you to respond. In turn, you think, "There she goes again. Doesn't let me get a word in edgewise—what a bitch!" Do your best to catch those thoughts, to stop them, and to write them down exactly.

Later, reread what you wrote and think about possible solutions. If you put your interactions and feelings in black and white, you will gain a better sense of your relationship's communication problems.

You must observe yourself. What is your position in these encounters? When the next conversation occurs, be the calm observer, which is a better position than being a silent, frustrated, or angry participant.

Are you interested and focused on your partner's replies? Do you two make eye contact? Is there a way you can jump in nicely to reroute or stop the annoying talk? For example, if your partner were a wealthy potential client and you wanted him or her to buy a car you were selling, how would you present yourself? Or if your partner were a beautiful and popular singer and you had written music you wanted that person to buy, what tactics would you use?

Experiment by listening carefully, set a time limit for yourself, and then do any of the following: ask a short question, nod in agreement, excuse yourself if you are unable to listen, indicate you will be right back, or take a quick walk to the bedroom or wherever. Take notes. If you expect change, you have to become the agent of change. By fully grasping and unraveling troubling talk, you are able to develop positive, specific alterations.

A Positive Solution

If, on the other hand, your partner agrees that she would like a better relationship, prepare not only for a temporary respite but also a U-turn back to confusing talk, which usually turns ugly.

Immediately take charge. To get your partner's full attention, tiptoe into the idea of improving the relationship. First, tell your partner that you love him or her; second, promise to remain positive.

Do not immediately forge ahead with your ideas. Resist any comments that deviate from improving the relationship. It is important not to get sidetracked and start interacting. Instead, set up the conversation as if it were a business meeting. Decide together on a time and place when you both will not be interrupted. You also need time lines to express thoughts, feelings, and possible solutions. For example, allow each person five, ten, or twenty minutes to air their grievances. Set your watch.

Be open to your partner's suggestions. Say supportive things like "that's a good idea," and be prepared for criticism. Take any criticism seriously and indicate you will think about it. By setting up a meeting, you have indicated that you want to know what your partner thinks and how he or she feels; acknowledge what your partner has to say.

You say, "I know I act that way sometimes." She says, "You always act that way." Do not respond in this case.

You could say, "We seem to have two different styles of talking. I know I can be curt. I like yes and no answers. You have a friendly way of sharing experiences."

You will need a series of these business meetings to untangle your communication history. You may have to set up guidelines; for example, decide together not to allow any criticizing, condemning, or complaining. Stay in a business mode. Solutions are the goal.

If you get the ball rolling on the above process, you will finally be traveling on the road to sharing thoughts, feelings, and experiences. You will establish a real relationship! Or you will see the relationship for what it is—ongoing confusion. Then you can make a conscious choice of whether to stay or go.

CHAPTER 24

Distortion

"I 'm going shopping," you say.

"You're always looking for ways to get away from me," says your husband.

This idea you ridicule because you've heard it before, but still it puts you on guard.

If you take his words seriously and you do go shopping, you must rush home, or he will be upset. His talk will engender either guilt (your husband comes home first, and you are neglecting him) or shame (you should not have a life of your own, or you struggle with control—he should decide what you do).

On the other hand, you might understand his words as manipulation, truth, or playfulness. Honestly, do you want to get away from him? Or is he a funny guy? "You know I was kidding. You make everything a big deal," he says. He pretends he did not mean anything and that you are misinterpreting his words. What is your truth? Clarify your thoughts, and take them seriously. In other words, start with yourself.

Pay close attention to the following items:

- You are puzzled and confused after a conversation.
- You often ask yourself, is it me or is it him?

- Situations, words, and feelings are out of proportion; they are either twisted and overly dramatic or made insignificant.
- Terms like *always*, *never*, *everyone*, and *nobody* are used.
- There is no gray area: experiences are good or bad.

Focus on your thinking. Do you or your partner twist and turn conversations into disturbing experiences in which your words snap rapport and inflame feelings instead of connecting you both? If so, when you are talking to your partner, take charge of yourself, and as best as you can, stay calm, think, and listen as a conscious observer.

Derek

Derek called for a marriage-counseling appointment. "My wife, Cathy, and I have been married awhile, and we seem to be sliding downhill; we have trouble talking without getting upset or fighting. Our habit is stupid because whatever we're talking about is never that important."

We agreed to meet in three days. Derek came alone and announced that his wife refused to join him, even though they had often talked about marriage counseling. He had assumed she would be pleased that he had set up an appointment.

Derek said, "I came alone to calm myself—if that's all right."

I assured him that marriage-counseling sessions often turned out to involve only one partner instead of two. "Your wife may change her mind, but if she does not, marriage counseling will be an opportunity for you to express thoughts and feelings to a person trained to help sort out partnership difficulties. We can solve your problems together, and I can show you how you can address them when you're alone.

"First of all, do you love your wife?"

He looked shocked. "Of course. I want the marriage."

Derek took a deep breath and settled down. Derek was forty-six, tall, and lanky. His body naturally tilted slightly forward. He wore large horn-rimmed glasses that gave him a thoughtful, owl-like look.

"My wife turns everything around. I can't have a regular conversation with her. Here's an example. I came home happy from a weekend conference, feeling inspired and full of interesting experiences. I'm a forensic psychologist.

"After I'm five minutes inside the door, my wife, Cathy, said, 'You never called.' She spoke with an accusatory voice; she did not give me a kiss or even ask how my trip had gone. I started to explain that my cell phone had lost service, but I couldn't get two words out before she launched into her woes, painting an ugly picture of being alone all weekend.

"Even though we agreed that I would go to the conference because it was important for my work, I think she resented the fact that I went, and when she was accusatory, I did feel guilty and responsible for her bad feelings. I think that was her point without saying it."

Derek spoke definitively, with the staccato beat of an army sergeant. He moved forward on the couch and continued. "Then her voice reached a fever pitch. She said I no longer loved her, that I was turned off by her.

"I was getting angry. Not that this sort of thing hasn't happened before, but for some reason, I wasn't prepared, and that kind of talk made me mad. I started to walk away, just to get relief, but I did not go far before she called me a 'fraidy cat,' among other nasty opinions.

"Isn't that ridiculous? Was I expected to listen without so much as a 'Hi, how are you?' What's more, she had the gall to get upset with me! Everything we talk about gets turned into something else."

"It is difficult to remain calm when faced with an emotionally charged person. It's not surprising that you respond to her emotional energy—emotions are contagious. Not only are they contagious, but also they may distort what you are hearing.

"The first step is to pay attention to yourself. Altering your listening patterns requires concentration, and you must be conscious of your styles of communicating and reacting, as well as your wife's styles. Are you doing anything to exacerbate the situation? The misinterpretation may be your experience, your understanding, or the feelings you generate and she responds to. You have been putting the onus of the problem on your wife.

"If you discover that you are doing the twisting, turning, and side-stepping, you are in luck because you can now change your method of interacting—or not. If your wife fails to understand, you can help by listening and responding differently and, therefore, change the way you communicate."

Change Tactics

"Settle down, quiet your mind, focus completely on your wife, and look at her eyes when you have something to say. Think about her positive qualities so that the nuances in your face represent pleasure. Remain calm, and stay on track with the points you make.

"Allow her to respond in any way. It is not necessary for you to point out that there is an error in her thinking or that she is twisting something you said. Your communication may not be clear, or the tone of your voice may be off putting. For example, perhaps you speak as though you have a podium in front of you and do not answer questions, or perhaps you mumble and deny mumbling. You may have a quizzical look on your face when she responds, making you appear as if you're thinking that whatever she had said was nonsense. The point is to be open minded. Listen to her as though she were a stranger.

"If you experiment without success and remain unable to calmly and pleasantly interact, don't worry: you are still gaining information about yourself and the relationship. It is possible that she cannot alter her pattern, that the neurons in her brain are set in a particular way. If that's the case, can you cope with her distortion?

Therapy Conclusion

Derek's wife did not join him in marriage counseling; however, he continued for six months, recognizing and altering the part he played in their interactions. He experimented with various communication methods.

Experimentation allowed Derek to work on taking control of himself and to view their interactions intellectually. He recognized and calmed his habitual emotional reactions of annoyance, confusion, frustration, and anger. As he calmed himself, he reported that his wife "seemed to be a different person." Their relationship changed because he had changed himself, and he felt calm and satisfied with their marriage.

CHAPTER 25
Deliberate Distortion

D istortion means exaggeration. When a person distorts something, he or she misleads or alters something out of its original shape, experience, or sound.

Conversational distortion is common. "I had such a wonderful time last night," says a friend.

"Really? You looked miserable."

"Well, maybe it wasn't *that* great."

Relationship distortion is usually subtle and slightly confusing, but in the case of Angela and Bill the distortion was obvious.

Angela and Bill

Angela's distortion of her husband Bill's personality had reached epidemic proportions and had become a serious threat to his standing in the family and the community. Angela was determined to establish her husband as mentally ill. She was not saying, as people often do, "That's crazy!" Instead, she was out to prove that her husband was crazy. Step by step, she built her case by magnifying and dramatizing his behavior and by taking his words out of context.

Fishing through the Internet for definitions, explanations, and other people's experiences, Angela attempted to carefully establish Bill as unstable and diagnosable, citing behaviors that fit the DSM V (*Diagnostic and Statistical Mental Health Manual*) category.

With an emotionally disturbed husband, Angela was off the hook. She could not be blamed for their marital problems. She was healthy, she was acting properly, and she was right. Bill was the problem, but at the same time, he could not help himself because she had "proved" he was mentally ill. She was settling in as the long-suffering masochist, letting both her family and his know about the pain she was enduring.

Angela's plan was a solution of sorts. It defined the situation and eased her mind while keeping her locked in a hostile environment.

Therapy

Bill, thirty-six, was a computer and stock-market whiz and had insisted on marriage counseling. Angela, also thirty-six, was a homemaker. She was unhappy about therapy but stated that she would help in any way she could. However, in their first session, she reported that Bill's mental state was their main problem.

Bill, about six foot four, stooped slightly as he and his wife found separate chairs in my office. Bill indicated his reason for seeking counseling was Angela's anger toward him.

Angela, who was rail thin and had trouble sitting still, said she had to let off steam. "Who wouldn't in my place? Occasionally, I get mad for having to live with a mental case. I build up so much frustration that I just blow up—but it only lasts about ten minutes. That's not much when what I put up with is considered."

Bill, hands in his lap, looked straight at me and disagreed. "She doesn't let off steam—she acts crazy. She screams, jumps up and down, and runs around while she puts me down. And this is done in front of the children. The woman cannot be contained.

"Angela is determined to make me crazy or make sure others know I'm seriously off the beam. She has informed everyone we know, including my sisters, that I have a diagnosable mental illness.

"She denies what I know is a fact. Her attitude makes me crazy. I feel like I've been accused of murder with circumstantial evidence, and it's out in the world as a fact. Our families wonder whether we're both crazy. Staying with Angela makes me wonder myself about my mental health. I try to stay away from her now. Anything I say can and will be used against me."

History
These two were at war. Their problems did not begin when they married; the groundwork had been laid years before. Both came from troubled backgrounds.

Angela
Angela's determination to prove her husband mentally ill was an unconscious attempt to re-create her parents' marriage. She portrayed her parents' relationship as good. She saw her mother as a kind but firm person; she thought her father was a wimp. Angela had no qualms stating that Bill was a weak and ineffective father. She portrayed herself as the powerful, long-suffering wife and mother.

Bill had a different take on her parents' relationship. "Angela's mother criticized Angela's father incessantly, but Angela ignored her mother's critical disposition."

Through gritted teeth, Angela said, "Despite my mother's *ways*, they have a very good relationship."

"Her parents have no social life because Angela's mother is impossible," said Bill. "Her constant bickering and harping is impossible for other people to tolerate, including her own family."

Bill

Bill, who had endured a physically and emotionally abusive father, did not recognize the beginning of Angela's abuse. When the relationship began, living with Angela was a pleasure compared with what he had been through as a child. Gradually, though, he recognized he was staying at the office for no good reason. He dreaded facing Angela at the end of the day. He became fearful of her moods and started to doubt himself all over again, as he had done as a child.

He tried to protect himself emotionally by withdrawing from Angela. At the same time, he began to question his sanity. Wanting to either cure himself or put to rest the notion that he was mentally ill, Bill sought therapy. Angela wanted therapy to prove she was right.

Emotionally, Angela and Bill were at an adolescent level and had so much developmental growing to do that the concept of trying to improve their life together had not even occurred to them.

Facts are necessary to untangle distortions. Since Bill's mental illness was Angela's main complaint, I suggested that both of them should take a battery of psychological tests as the first step in their therapy. Bill thought that testing and continuing therapy were good ideas. Angela refused testing and left therapy after two sessions. She called two months later and left this message on my answering machine: "This is Angela…I found a *good* therapist who believes in me."

If you illuminate distortion, you gain the opportunity to unravel the confusion. In the case of Bill and Angela, the unraveling opportunity came and went as the relationship dissolved, and they hit a concrete communication barrier. Their divorce proceedings began and ended in rancor that did not solve anything; instead, their ill will exacerbated their angry feelings for each other.

Managing Distortions

Developing a communication style can be difficult. It requires writing, thinking, and having serious talks with an objective person.

Once you tease out specific examples, you have choices: stop and alter interactions or acknowledge that crazy communication will never end.

View the following ideas as if they are as important as identifying, verifying, and tracking stock indexes:

1. When you are confused by an interaction, write down exactly what was said. Do not depend on your memory. When you talk to your partner about the conversation, you need facts. Without facts, you will spin off into another distortion. (This might happen even with facts.)

2. Break down the words into fact or distortion. List each fact and each distortion separately.

3. Tell your partner you want to have a discussion. Set up privacy, establish an exact time of day or night, and limit the time of the appointment. Your partner may ask what the meeting is about, reply that the subject is communication confusion. Refuse to enter a discussion at that moment in time; it will not be constructive.

4. Refuse to argue. If one person refuses to argue, arguing becomes impossible.

5. Plan to have these talks on a regular basis, once a week or twice a month. Be persistent, or your partner will not get it. That is, he

or she must know you are serious and, through repetition, will hopefully grasp what you are saying.

6. Your job is to listen carefully and to stay on track.
7. Do not be discouraged. Time and energy are required to think through distorted conversations and to stay focused.

Dissociation is another communication style that produces confusion and unhappiness.

CHAPTER 26
Dissociation

Three words characterize life with a person who dissociates: *evaporate*, *dissipate*, and *elusive*. Like a cloud that rolls by, words evaporate and context disappears. Dissociation is childish. People who dissociate often say things like "I didn't do it" or "what are you talking about? I didn't say that." Responsibility for words and behavior is denied. Previous communication drops through their minds like a sieve.

To dissociate is when a person, rather than directly face a problem, mentally looks the other way, and the problem disappears as though it had never risen. If your spouse says, "I didn't say that," you will be stopped dead in your tracks unless you have recorded the exact words of what he or she previously said. The conversation will go nowhere unless you keep a record.

The reaction does not make sense because on the one hand, your partner remembers interactions with friends and retains huge amounts of information related to various things, such as a career performance, stock-market indexes, and trivia from various sports. On the other hand, when it comes to relationship conversations, situations, or emotions, his or her mind is blank.

Your dissociative partner can never be pinned down. If you question your partner, you receive denial about what was just said or done and an assurance that your interpretation was incorrect. You become confused. Your partner is appalled that you are making such a big deal out of nothing. Given this reaction, you are shaken and befuddled and feel invisible.

Dissociation is a shortsighted, shallow, surface life, a state that resembles a person with a lobotomy. It would be different if the reply was "oh, did I say that? I can't remember."

A person who dissociates will make a statement, and ten minutes later, an hour later, or a day later, that person will declare opposite feelings or ideas. When you report feeling puzzled and want clarification, the person who dissociates knows what they have not said and, consequently, cannot alter or give up words or behaviors that are not in their head at that moment in time.

In other words, thought is in a different compartment now, and the door on the other compartment has clanged shut. The mind is blank. What are you talking about? Some would call people who dissociate liars, but dissociating indicates conflict rather than fabrication; it is a form of compartmentalization. A blatant example is a minister who teaches moral values but, at the same time, embezzles funds.

Psychologically splitting and dissociating go hand in hand. Splitting is similar to having a separate box in your head for events, another box for relationships, another box for cooking, and so forth. When a person moves from one box to another, the new box's door opens and the last box is forgotten as the dissociating or splitting brain moves from one situation to another.

Managing Dissociation Versus Forgetfulness or Lying

Larry's and Jeannie's remembrances of talks and events always ended with the same frustrating results. Jeannie said, "Larry cannot remember any discussion, regardless of importance. I can't stand it. Even with small things, like a plan to go to the store at half past three, he will say, 'Oh, I thought you said four o'clock.'

"It's like there's a hole in his head, and anything I say drops through and disappears. It's infuriating. He's sweet and then suddenly mean. I'm angry, and I don't know what to do. I'm confused. His behavior feels deliberate, so I want to retaliate and take action. Sometimes I do; then I feel ashamed. Larry is a smart man, but around me, he acts brain dead."

Solution

"Here is what you can do," I said. "You are neither upset nor angry—you are calm. Let your partner know that because he forgets problems and situations, you do not. Talk in a comforting voice, and indicate what the struggles about who said what, when, and how are over. You probably cannot lay the matter to rest when you first discuss the issue, so you must suggest in a calm, quiet voice that since there is a question about what goes on between you two, perhaps an electronic recording device would solve the problem. He may object; nevertheless, buy one and use it.

"Do not let the matter drop. Do not get mad. Be persistent. Since he is capable of remembering other situations, have patience. Try to determine whether he recognizes the importance of his forgetfulness with you and whether he wants to change his thought processes. Change requires time. Your job is to beam him onto your wavelength by attending to his inattention.

"If he chooses not to take you seriously, you must change your thought patterns, stop frustrated thinking, and view interactions as concrete. This is it forever; you are a captive of his dissociating brain. You do have choices: counseling, acceptance, or separation.

"Personalization is another personality style that muddies the waters of communication and often unravels a satisfactory relationship."

CHAPTER 27
Personalization

To interpret and evaluate people with your experience is automatic. To interpret, evaluate, and believe that their words pertain to you when there is no evidence is personalization.

These experiences should sound familiar: Someone across the street laughs, and you think that person is laughing at you. Some of your friends are speaking quietly out of earshot, so you assume they are talking about you. Maybe they are, but unless they tell you, your thought is a personalized guess. When your wife is disgruntled, your children disagreeable, or your friend snappy, you may feel somehow responsible and think, "Uh oh, what did I do?"

The operative word is *belief*. A fleeting thought is simply a thought that comes to mind; *believing* your thought is personalization. Personalization is neither rational nor intelligent. It's like looking at a tree, and because you cannot see the roots, you declare the tree to be a statue.

Living with a personalizer is frustrating and generates anger; these people do not have the ability to grasp their reality as being distorted. To a person who personalizes, the personalizer's reality is the only reality, and despite evidence to the contrary, he or she is always right.

Ann and Kirk

Casually dressed for her first marriage-counseling session, Ann, thirty-four, was an attractive housewife. She said, "BC—that is, before children—I was a career woman."

Her husband, Kirk, a thirty-six-year-old, reported that he was an at-home, on-time, no-drinking-or-carousing kind of guy. He never even considered smoking marijuana as a teenager. In other words, Kirk presented himself as steady as a rock, and he held no interest in any extra-curricular activities. Ann concurred.

This information was the forerunner to their problem. Ann told me that she had issues with a neighbor whom she believed Kirk found attractive. "Our neighbor, Cindy, is flamboyant and flirtatious, and although Kirk assures me that he is totally uninterested in her, I see an attraction there.

"We went to a neighborhood party, as did Cindy, who was dressed in an outfit that looked like a Halloween costume to me, or maybe she was just plain trying to be sexy. She had on a very short, tight skirt with a fit-ted bodice or something, and she kept talking to Kirk. It made me sick."

Kirk looked distressed. "Ann assumes that her thoughts of seduction are correct, and she acts as if that belief has been written in stone. No one is seducing anyone. I don't know where she gets these ideas. Our neighbor dresses like a floozy, and she talked to every man at the party."

"Well," said Ann, staring at Kirk, "what about when I went to pick up Josie [their daughter] at Cindy's house? She was wearing see-through pants because she had thought *you* were going to pick up our daughter."

"I can't help what she wears, can I?"

Again, Ann embraced the idea that Kirk was a coconspirator. "You answered the phone when she called. She is definitely interested in you. I can tell."

Kirk was beginning to get agitated and raised his voice. "So what? I am not even slightly attracted to or interested in her." Then Kirk turned to me. "You can see how we get nowhere. No matter what I say or how I act, Ann is determined she is right.

"She does it about other things as well. For example, she is dead set on the idea that my father doesn't like her. Ann is a very likable person. She is normally sweet and nice to people. My dad thinks she's great, but she simply won't accept that fact; consequently, she is always on edge when he comes over."

Besides the obvious personal unhappiness, Ann's personalization also got her into trouble in their neighborhood. Kirk said, "One August evening, neighbors were outside chatting, and Ann made a point of finding Cindy. In a loud voice, she proceeded to inform her that she wore slutty clothes and was overly flirtatious. Then she told Cindy to stop talking to me."

Kirk groaned when he was finished with the story. He said he felt furious, embarrassed, and totally frustrated. "I told her she was jealous, and that made her angry, but the truth is that she hasn't actually been jealous about other women. She just gets weird ideas in her mind, and as a consequence of her behavior, I refuse to attend neighborhood parties."

After Kirk's rendition of the confrontation, Ann appeared chagrined. In a half-hearted defense, she said, "Maybe I was too assertive, but I think I needed to confront Cindy. I can't let her get away with chasing my husband."

Personalization Specifics

"You cannot help putting your spin on events," I said, "but you need to recognize that these ideas are simply coming from your point of view— you are bringing everything into your orbit. You are totally subjective, and other people's perspectives are either wrong or invalid. You cannot get past yourself when you personalize."

When Ann personalized, she did the following:

- Automatically assumed that whatever was going on with Kirk had to do with her.
- Felt way too much in reaction to others. She ignored or was missing an intellectual filter. If Kirk was sick, she was sick. Kirk had to dumb down his feelings or monitor what he said to prevent Ann from taking his comments as a personal affront.
- She transferred her thoughts to Kirk or others. If she thought something like "he knows I didn't mean that" without verbalizing it, she would assume Kirk was thinking the same thing.

Not a pretty picture, but when you are living with a person who personalizes, you can chalk up their reactions to a brain neuron that malfunctions. If you feel the need to confront your partner, you can expect an argument indicating you are wrong.

Immediate Solution

"Stay steady and calm with your version of your truth, which is easier said than done," I said to Kirk. "Arguing will not produce positive results. The issue is that you need to learn to handle two versions of reality."

Long-Term Solution

"We are all defensive at times; we need our defenses. Defenses are meant to protect, not compromise, our lives. Understanding your defensiveness after a marital disturbance will help you control and alter future reactions to Ann's accusations and to view her ideas as those of an active imagination.

"Communication problems that are built into a personality or are the result of developed defenses do not change without a major mental upheaval. The only change that will occur is your recognition that Ann's behavior is written in stone. It is in your best interest to find a solution that suits you.

"Your expectations of how Ann should behave or how she should respond sets you up for disappointment, agitation, and anger. Approach Ann with the same consideration, kindness, and respect that you would give to a stranger. Remain calm.

"Do not enter into a 'who is right' discussion. You are yanking each other down to the lowest common denominator when you struggle to determine who is right. Instead, take on the role of the understanding friend, ally, and coworker—take whichever role feels comfortable. Respectfully listen to her ideas. Let her know that that is what she thinks, and then insert your own insight while remaining calm, cool, and collected.

"As difficult as it is, stay steady.

"Can you stop frustration that flashes instantaneously into your mind? No. However, the minute you recognize the frustration, let it go. It is an old response that upsets you for no reason. It's like stomping your feet like a baby because you want to touch the stove. Stomping feet get babies nowhere, and frustration won't do anything, except cause you distress. You cannot stop Ann's talk or reactions, but you can continue to be rational and, in no uncertain terms, repeat your point of view.

"Ann has self-esteem issues that can be addressed and resolved in therapy—if she is able to absorb ideas that are different from her own. In the meantime, because marriage is a seesaw, soothe yourself with the knowledge that in an intimate relationship, one person's words and actions have a powerful effect on the other, whether the words are immediately acknowledged or not.

The Plan

"Tolerance should not be forced, and one person should not have to take the role of peacemaker or mediator in a relationship, but in reality, that is often the case. You walk the line between giving your partner respect and respecting yourself. Since you chose your partner, you are respecting your own choice when you, at the least, use good manners and are polite and friendly. It is in your best interest to bring happiness into your life by taming those resentful, cranky, or angry impulses.

"But, if unhappiness in the relationship persists—even when you have discovered, defined, and found a variety of solutions for difficult problems, communication styles, or personality characteristics—another avenue is available."

Part 5 contains a seven-day, step-by-step plan to shake up common habits of couples. The plan will put your relationship on an upward trajectory.

PART FIVE

Seven-Day Action Plan

n the first four sections, I explored overt and covert anger issues in depth, and each scenario was followed by possible solutions. Part 5 details a seven-day action plan designed to spot specific positive behaviors touched on in previous sections.

By taking charge of yourself, consciously focusing on each step, and actively incorporating this seven-day guide, you will dramatically improve not only your intimate partnership but also every relationship in your life.

Seven Requirements for Resolving Angry Relationships

The seven steps essential for a good relationship are not unknown to you. In fact, during your courtship, they were your raison d'etre, the positive focus of your life. You viewed your loved one with total positive regard and overlooked (in fact, might have admired) his or her quirks and unusual behavior. You were in a love zone.

As you have seen in the first four parts, the love zone often becomes a war zone. If peace, not war, is your goal, proceed.

Each day for seven days, focus on the following steps, one at a time:

1. Develop listening skills.
2. Forgive the past.

3. Think positively.
4. Speak positively.
5. Verbalize emotions positively.
6. Compliment your partnership.
7. Generate solutions.

Day 1: Listening Skills

Consciously relax your mind and body. Prepare to eliminate any negative, judgmental thoughts that come to mind.

Today, you will focus on your partner: listen, seriously note what is said, and thoughtfully respond. Put yourself in the other person's shoes. No uh huh or umm's.

Today, you must remember that whatever your partner says is his or her understanding of the world. Even if the communication is addressed to you or seems to be about you, the ideas belong to your mate. The words may or may not be relevant. Setting your partner straight is irrelevant.

Depersonalize. If you are having an emotional reaction or have a powerful need to express an opposite opinion, a denial, or a different point of view, write it down and wait for ten days. After ten days, if you still need expression, you will share your opinion at that time.

Your job is to rephrase what your partner says and to indicate you are paying attention. You are interested in how his or her mind works.

If your partner lets you know you misunderstood, fine. It is possible that you are unconsciously editing an opinion. Thank your mate. View misunderstandings as educational.

You must be willing, eager, and available to listen. Pretend you are talking to a stranger who speaks peculiarly and softly. You have to pay close attention to understand. You are open, nonjudgmental, accepting, compassionate, and cooperative.

Day 2: Forgive and Forget The Past

Day 2 is forgiveness day. Forgive your misdeeds and your partner's; let the past go. You cannot relive the past and, more importantly, educating your significant other by dredging up historical miseries is like spitting in the wind.

You may think something like "she said I'm stupid. She also embarrassed me in front of my boss and once slapped my face. I'll never be able to forgive her for those insults." If you don't learn to forgive and move on, you will create your own emotional prison.

Your can make both of you miserable by keeping the past alive or you can use the hurts as learning tools. Your goal is to turn away from the blame game, put aside bitterness and retribution, and forgive.

Consciously dedicate this day to replacing ugly, mean-spirited thoughts about the past with a mind-set that is calm and satisfied, one that can bring happiness. When you realize that everything is fundamentally a matter of perception and that you can control your mind, you go from dwelling on resentment to forgiveness.

Remember that when distressing incidents occurred in the past, you and your partner were different people. At a later time, if you cannot let go of an incident from the past, you should take the information to a psychologist and therapeutically work it out.

Dismiss and forgive negative thoughts, words, and behaviors from the past.

Day 3: Speak Positively

On day 3, every word to your partner should be positive. Speak about what you like. Show appreciation. Use sticky notes to remind yourself to speak positively; place them in your car, at your desk, or at wherever you spend your days and nights. Speak in a loving, positive manner toward your mate.

Communication confusion often results from discrepancies between the message sent and the message received. When your spouse speaks, your job is to ask for clarification and to acknowledge his or her thoughts and feelings. If your partner says something that surprises or puzzles you, ask for clarification instead of supplying your own meaning. Ask questions without voice inflections that suggest you know better.

In a positive tone and upbeat manner, mirror what you hear your partner saying. Resist giving advice, and do not verbalize your interpretation or assume the worst. Reflect on the content and emotion of your partner's words as though you were translating a foreign language. Your translation may feel or sound awkward; do not let that stop you. The goal is to clarify in a pleasant, positive manner.

The second you begin to react by bickering, arguing, defending yourself, or disputing your partner's words, stop! That behavior was not effective in the past, and it will not be effective now. Find some truth in your partner's words, despite whether the content seems wrong or ridiculous to you.

Eliminate hostility from your conversations. If your partner points out that you seem angry, hostile, or sarcastic, do not put on an innocent act or feel that you have to rebut the statement. Take it like a grown-up, and say thanks for the observation, no matter what thoughts or feelings you have.

Use your mate's observations to help you. We cannot see or hear ourselves objectively. Depersonalize as though you were listening to a stranger. You may be presenting yourself in a manner that is not in your best interest.

Inner negative dialogue will sway attention from your goal, causing your resolve to waver. Plan on it. Simply replace negative thoughts with positive thoughts. Remind yourself that this is a seven-day project and that you can do anything for seven days. Do not let yourself down.

Day 4: Think Positively

Life will reflect your choice to think positively. Happiness within is reflected by happiness without. Think about what you are thinking about. You can control the ongoing dialogue in your mind; you can think anything you want to think. This minute, think about the positive experience you want in your relationship.

Squelch any negative thoughts, no matter how real they seem or how important it seems to express the thoughts. For example, you may think something like "I'm doing all the changing here—she is doing nothing." Yes, you are changing, and that means you have control of yourself. Or you may think something like "he always reacts like that—that makes me mad!" Remember that you are in charge of your thought processes. No other person can *make* you mad.

When you catch yourself thinking negatively, stop. Think again. Replace a negative idea immediately with love or, if you can't muster loving thoughts, any neutral, positive thought will do.

Expect old thoughts to pop into your mind, but do not speak about the past. It's over. Discussing it one more time won't change anything.

Do not mentally edit anything by thinking something like "this can't be done" or "there he goes again—it's hopeless" or "this won't work." Negative, judgmental thoughts will sabotage your goal. They are fragmented old thoughts that will become real if you make them real.

Calm Down And Stop Negative Dialogue

Maximize opportunities to stay on target with your happiness goals. At the same time, be aware that at times you will regress and that opposing thoughts will surface. When old thoughts and feelings enter your mind, take a deep breath, and bring focused consciousness to your goal for the day. Historical negative thoughts and agitated feelings will disappear when you take charge of yourself and deliberately let them go—new thoughts may last for only a moment, allowing old worry, agitation, or negative thoughts to slip back into place. Catch the negative thoughts, and tell yourself that if they are historical, they are not real.

You have been communicating your entire life and have developed thought pathways in your brain that may not be positive or solution oriented. Be patient with yourself and your partner. You are in an experimental time capsule. Right now, you are a robot following instructions.

What is real at this moment in time is your goal to take charge of your thoughts. You are focused on thinking and speaking positively rather than on reacting to thoughts that come to mind. You handled your thoughts today and made sure they were upbeat. If not, note what went wrong and rehearse ideal thoughts and words. Stay on track.

Day 5: Positive Feelings

Cement these thoughts in place: You feel great today. You are happy that you are a thinking person who has decided to improve life by changing thoughts and speaking positively. You can handle anything that comes your way because you are relaxed and feel good. You are going to continue feeling good all day and all night. The thoughts you think and the words you speak are uplifting to you and everyone around you.

Feelings are fueled by thoughts. You rely on feelings to feed yourself information. At any moment, a thinking glitch may occur, switching you to an old negative-dialogue path with feelings of depression, anxiety, anger, or any number of sad, sorrowful feelings. No problem.

Catch the thoughts as quickly as you can, stop your mind, and replace negativity with positive feelings immediately.

When you are feeling uneasy and unhappy, you rummage around until you dredge up a reason. You think thoughts like "I think the marriage is falling apart. I hate the way George talks to me" or "I'm afraid she might leave, despite everything I'm doing." Will those feelings and thoughts help you? No.

Instead, acknowledge the feelings and deliberately let them go with a command to yourself that you are not going to feel sad or bad at that moment. Put the feelings in an imaginary bag, and imagine throwing it into the garbage.

Conversely, it is important to express feelings openly and freely. Feelings are a part of the human experience. But because they come to mind does not mean that you need to do any of the following: (1) entertain them, (2) use them as an excuse to pout, withdraw, or act aggressively, or (3) indicate you know how your spouse feels, which causes you to feel ten times worse.

I am not suggesting you bottle yourself up forever. It is important to be authentic. If you feel angry with your mate for present or past words or behaviors, get out a pen and paper or use your computer to express negative feelings, and move those feelings out of your system (and do not leave that information lying around). Your job at that moment in time is to focus on positive thoughts and behavior and to eliminate depressed, negative feelings.

When you feel tense or nervous and the feeling will not go away, shake it off by exercising. Any form of exercise for an hour will eliminate stressed feelings. And do not moan about the time it takes to exercise. We find time to do whatever is a priority. You know that tension and nervousness affect your relationship and that you become self-absorbed when you feel miserable.

Do not be discouraged! This is an experiment, and experiments take time and focus. Every hour on the hour, tell yourself how energized and positive you feel. Rome was not built in a day, and neither was your relationship.

Day 6: Compliment Your Partner

Today, once every hour, take one minute to think of one specific positive partner attribute—such as physical or intellectual attributes, parenting skills, or things she or he does for you. Then speak about those qualities and be specific. For example, a wife should not simply say to her husband that he is a good father. Instead, she should say something like "when I hear you talking to Johnny about his skateboarding, he lights right up. I can feel the love and respect between you."

To compliment your partner sincerely gives a gift to yourself as well. You feed your soul when you think and speak of others in ways that uplift their spirits.

If complimenting your partner feels awkward or insincere, you must overcome that feeling. Stay on target. If you do not feel like complimenting your partner, ask yourself what the big deal is. There are things at home or on the job that you might not feel like doing; still, you take care of your responsibilities. Your job today is to verbalize your partner's positive attributes.

At first, you may struggle to present compliments or even get them out of your mouth. On top of your discomfort, you may have to deal with your partner's surprise, discomfort, disbelief, or questioning tone.

If your spouse enjoys a compliment, that is great! If not, your purpose is not to dissect or evaluate your partner's reply. You will know when you hit a bull's-eye with a compliment. Like anything, the more experience you have, the better you will do.

How many times did you compliment your partner? One compliment is oil in the machinery of your relationship. Tomorrow, add to your compliment score.

Compliments are positive. Remind yourself that your job is to think, feel, and act positively.

Day 7: Generate Solutions

Today, situate yourself in a concrete, businesslike mind-set. If a problem arises and it must be solved during this seven-day time frame, creatively generate several possible solutions, and ask your partner to do the same.

You have good ideas, but you do not know best. Be willing to be wrong. Cooperate. Look for peaceful, mediated solutions, and doing so requires that your ideas and your partner's be considered.

Generating solutions requires a businesslike mind-set.

1. Determine ahead of time that the discussion will be calm, cool, and collected. If either of you becomes agitated, call a time-out and resume later.
2. Assign a specific time to talk about the problem, and talk only about the problem at that time.
3. Stop talking when twenty minutes have passed, no matter where you are in the solution process.
4. At the end of twenty minutes, write down the solutions you have reached, and schedule another meeting.
5. Listen carefully. Don't allow any interruptions.

You are presenting possibilities. If your solution is batted down, pout for a second, and then move on. Do not make quips like "well, you have such great ideas, but I don't notice you solving the problem." Do not verbalize this type of thinking. You simply must let it pass through your mind.

Remember that every problem has a solution.

Additional Ideas
Practice

During your seven-day project, continually remind yourself to keep up the conscious programming. Practice, practice, practice! Don't let your mind drift into mental mayhem. Concentrate your energy on positively changing your thoughts and feelings.

Plan on receiving resistance not only from your partner but also from yourself. When you hear thoughts that are in opposition to your stated goal, clear them out. Be prepared for your mind to fragment. Expect habit-driven mental configurations to segue into worry, doubt, anxiety, depression, and fearfulness. Resistant new thoughts may jump into your mind to fight the seven secrets.

View your mind as a computer: you can delete all thoughts and feelings that sabotage the positive seven-day goals. The worst mistake you can make now is to relax into old habits.

Misleading Behavior

If you think that you do not want to mislead your spouse by acting positively when you actually have thoughts that the relationship may not work or separation may be in the future, remember your partner is a grown-up. You are not responsible for his or her behavior. Your partner will react in whatever manner is right for him or her.

The fact is that you are in the relationship right now. It does not make sense that you have to be distant or negative to protect your spouse from disappointment in case the relationship ultimately does not work.

If you act cheerful and positive, you will feel better, and the people around you will feel better. If you do ultimately separate from your partner, you will make the future relationship amicable by putting your best foot forward right now.

What if Nothing in the Marriage Changes?

At the end of the seven days, the worst that can happen is that you will feel disappointed, sad, angry, or some other kind of pain—that is, you will feel what you have felt before. Even disappointment is helpful. It helps clarify what is and is not possible.

Your relationship is like a heart condition: wherever you go and whatever you do, you will never be free. The rhythmic, soothing beats or the erratic, angry beats of your relationship affect every part of your life.

Now you see that you have options: you can either stay the same, continue to enhance the partnership, or realize that it is time to stop the struggle and move on in your life.

You choose.

ABOUT THE AUTHOR

Carol L. Rhodes, PhD, has spent thirty-five years as a clinical psychologist as well as a marital and family therapist. She has given advice through numerous self-help columns and interviews with the media. In addition to *Anger: Surviving Toxic Relationships*, Rhodes is also the author of *Affair: Emergency Tactics* and *I'm Just Not Happy*. Along with Dr. Norman Goldner, she cowrote *Why Women and Men Don't Get Along*.